The Anglo-Boer War
in 100
OBJECTS

The Anglo-Boer War

in 100
OBJECTS

War Museum of the Boer Republics

FRONTLINE
BOOKS

First published in Great Britain in 2018 by
Frontline Books
An imprint of
Pen & Sword Books Ltd
Yorkshire – Philadelphia

First published in South Africa in 2017 by
JONATHAN BALL PUBLISHERS

ISBN 978-1-52673-403-7

*Every effort has been made to trace the copyright
holders and to obtain their permission for the use of
copyright material. The publishers apologise for any
errors or omissions and would be grateful to be notified
of any corrections that should be incorporated in future
editions of this book.*

Cover by Simon Richardson
Design and typesetting by Chris McClain
Translation by Angela Voges
Editing by Alfred LeMaitre
Proofreading by Kathleen Sutton
Index by Sanet le Roux
Printed and bound in India by Replika Press Pvt. Ltd.
(M) Sdn. Bhd, Malaysia
Set in Adobe Caslon Pro 10pt

For more information on our books please visit
www.frontline-books.com
or email info@frontlinebooks.com

For a complete list of Pen & Sword titles
please contact
PEN & SWORD BOOKS LTD
47 Church Street, Barnsley, South Yorkshire,
S70 2AS, England
E-mail: enquiries@pen-and-sword.co.uk
Website: www.pen-and-sword.co.uk
Or
PEN AND SWORD BOOKS
1950 Lawrence Rd, Havertown, PA 19083, USA
E-mail: Uspen-and-sword@casematepublishers.com
Website: www.penandswordbooks.com

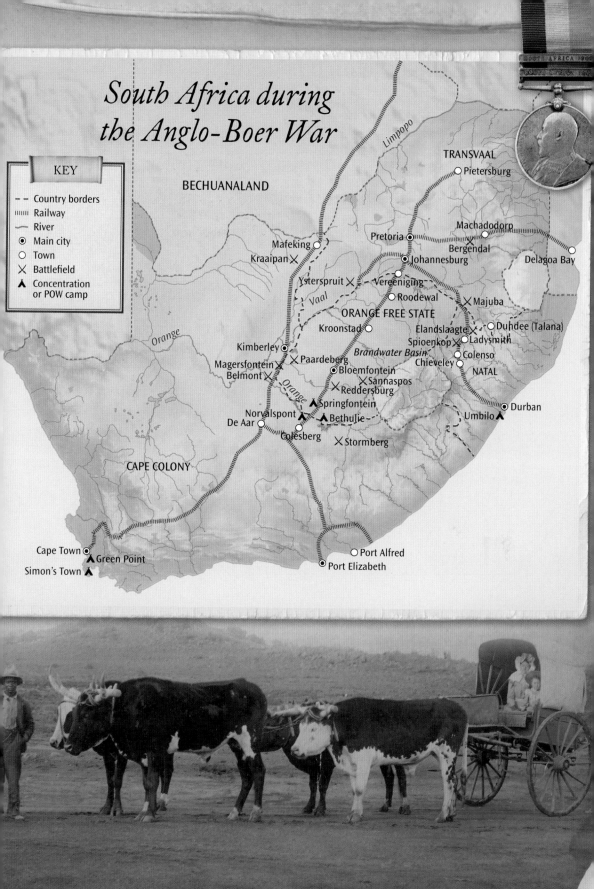

South Africa during the Anglo-Boer War

KEY

- – – Country borders
- ||||| Railway
- —— River
- ◉ Main city
- ○ Town
- ✕ Battlefield
- ⚓ Concentration or POW camp

BECHUANALAND

TRANSVAAL

Limpopo

○ Pietersburg

Machadodorp ○

Pretoria ◉ |||||||| Bergendal

Mafeking ○

Kraaipan ✕

◉ Johannesburg

Delagoa Bay ○

Ysterspruit ✕ ✕ Vereeniging

Vaal

✕ Roodewal

✕ Majuba

ORANGE FREE STATE

Kroonstad ○

Elandslaagte ✕ ○ Duhdee (Talana)

Spioenkop ✕ ⚓ Ladysmith

Kimberley ◉

Brandwater Basin

○ Colenso

Magersfontein ✕ ✕ Paardeberg

Chieveley ✕ ○

Belmont ✕

◉ Bloemfontein

NATAL

Orange

✕ Sannaspos

✕ Reddersburg

○ Durban

Norvalspont ⚓ Springfontein

Umbilo ⚓

De Aar ○ ⚓ Bethulie

Colesberg ○

✕ Stormberg

CAPE COLONY

Cape Town ◉

⚓ Green Point

○ Port Alfred

Simon's Town ⚓

◉ Port Elizabeth

Contents

Foreword

The War Museum of the Boer Republics in Bloemfontein tells the story of the Anglo-Boer War, waged in South Africa between 1899 and 1902. The largest conflict ever to have taken place on South African soil, it was fought between Queen Victoria's Great Britain and the two Boer republics: the South African Republic (Zuid-Afrikaansche Republiek, or ZAR) under President Paul Kruger and the Republic of the Orange Free State under President Marthinus Steyn.

The chief causes of the war were the discovery of gold in the South African Republic and British imperial ambitions. In British historiography, the Anglo-Boer War – also known as the South African War – is frequently described as one of the colonial era's more decisive events. It not only signalled the end of Great Britain's imperialism, but also taught the colonial power countless military lessons that stood it in good stead during the First World War.

The Anglo-Boer War was also an important turning point in South Africa's history. In one way or another, it affected a multitude of South Africans of different cultural backgrounds, age groups, genders and races. Its effects on the political, economic and social landscape echoed long after 1902. The trauma of the concentration camps, where thousands of black and white women and children lost their lives, shaped the Afrikaner psyche for generations and fed the burgeoning Afrikaner nationalism that put the National Party into power in 1948 and ushered in the apartheid era.

After the war, Afrikaners sought a tangible way to remember and commemorate. This led to the formation of the War Museum of the Boer Republics in 1931. During and after the war, many

people clung to objects that symbolised the war or the hardships that they had endured in it. Many of these objects have been donated to the museum over the past few decades; today, the museum houses almost 50 000 objects – from photographs, documents, artworks, prisoner-of-war art and philately to firearms, artillery, medals, textiles, furniture and objects in many other categories.

Given that the War Museum is the world's only museum about the Anglo-Boer War, and that many of its objects are not on display, this publication, which singles out 100 main objects from the museum's collection, as well as 216 secondary objects, was compiled not only to present an overview of salient wartime objects but also to serve as a valuable source of information for local and international collectors alike.

Importantly, the publication does not set out to be an academic treatise. Rather, it is a concise synopsis of the war through the 100 main objects, and one, we hope, that will pique readers' curiosity and broaden their background knowledge about the war.

The first of its kind in South Africa, this publication takes the reader on a chronological journey through the war, but also speaks, thematically, to these sorrowful events. It also honours all the South Africans who entrusted their treasured keepsakes to the War Museum.

This book is a realisation of one of the War Museum's greatest ideals. The director of the War Museum wishes to thank the author, publisher and all colleagues who were involved in the project for their contribution to this unique enrichment of Anglo-Boer War history.

TOKKIE PRETORIUS
Director: War Museum of the Boer Republics
Bloemfontein, South Africa

A Free State commando at the outbreak of the war.

Introduction

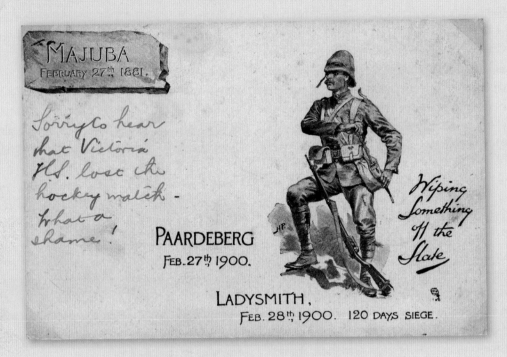

MAJUBA
FEBRUARY 27th 1881.

Sorry to hear
that Victoria
H.S. lost the
hockey match –
what a
shame!

PAARDEBERG
FEB. 27th 1900.

Wiping
Something
off the
Slate

LADYSMITH,
FEB. 28th 1900. 120 DAYS SIEGE.

A British postcard with a personal and a political message.

The *Anglo-Boer War in 100 Objects* traces the course of the Anglo-Boer War in 10 chapters through rare objects from the collection of the War Museum of the Boer Republics that link to specific events in the conflict. The selection of objects ranges from a British lance, a bonnet with bullet holes in it and rare *veldponde* (coins) to a British Rice blockhouse and garrison hospital on the premises of the War Museum. A brief summary accompanies each of the 100 objects, which aims to contextualise further the events or individuals with which the objects are associated. The 100 main objects are indicated by a symbol (☞) placed at the end of the relevant caption.

Events such as the Battle of Magersfontein or the Siege of Ladysmith are, by nature, challenging to reduce to a few words. Core facts, therefore, are the primary focus, with further background supplied in longer sections. Using the War Museum's databases and systems, we have attempted to provide as much information as possible about each item. In addition, each main item is further supplemented by historical photographs, documents, artworks or other related objects. To draw readers nearer to an event or person, some quotations are also included.

Selecting the objects was this publication's greatest challenge. In this, the War Museum was guided by what was available and which objects would illustrate moments in the war most effectively. Not all battles could be covered: the focus is on decisive battles such as the ones at Sannaspos in the Orange Free State (the guerrilla phase's first battle) and Bergendal (Dalmanutha) in the eastern Transvaal, in which all the Long Tom siege guns were brought into simultaneous service. As far as possible, we have avoided complex military terminology and endeavoured to keep the text accessible.

Each chapter portrays an important facet of the war, as the brief sketch that follows shows. The first chapter, 'War Clouds Gather', gives a brief overview of the two republics and discusses events in the run-up to the war, such as the Jameson Raid and the failed Bloemfontein Conference. Chapter 2, 'Initial Battles and Sieges', describes the siege phase of the war, and focuses on the early battles, particularly in Natal.

'Black Week and the Fall of the Republics' tells of the paralysing setbacks that British forces experienced within a single week in December 1899 – but also of how the British military regrouped to occupy first Bloemfontein and then Pretoria a handful of months later.

'Mauser vs Lee-Metford' discusses the warring parties' fighting forces and arsenal. 'Medical Services' shows the full extent to which medical care was still in its infancy during the war, and the chapter that follows it, The War's Cast of

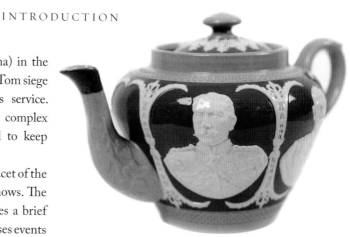

Fancy a patriotic cup of tea ... with Lord Kitchener?

Characters, identifies a number of important personalities on both Boer and British sides.

In 'The Guerrilla Phase', the spotlight falls on the war's protracted second phase, in which the so-called Bittereinders persisted in their fight. This chapter also offers a glimpse of life in the field for the commandos and for the government at large of the ZAR. The pain of the war dominates the 'Scorched Earth' chapter, which describes Lord Kitchener's scorched-earth policy and the concentration camps.

'Prisoners of War' describes life in Boer prisoner-of-war camps from St Helena to Ceylon (Sri Lanka), and displays some of the beautiful handicrafts made by the prisoners. 'Peace and the Post-war Years' discusses the peace negotiations and how, more than a century later, the war lives on in memory. One of this chapter's most notable objects is the pen used by Lord Kitchener to sign the Peace of Vereeniging, the agreement that brought the war to an end.

We trust that these objects, so dear to many of us, will bring a greater understanding of the Anglo-Boer War and its effects.

JOHAN VAN ZŸL
Editor

British soldiers guide a blindfolded burgher to their camp.

After the Boer republics sent an ultimatum to Britain in October 1899, hundreds of Uitlanders, individuals of foreign extraction, hastily left Johannesburg out of fear that they might be caught up in the looming war.

THE WAR
A SCRAMBLE FO
IN OPEN

CHAPTER 1

War Clouds Gather

BARNETT & C°

TRUCKS

The Republic of the Orange Free State

In 1652, the Dutch East India Company – a Dutch chartered company – established a trading post at the Cape of Good Hope, on the southern tip of Africa, and controlled it for more than 140 years.

The British occupied the Cape between 1795 and 1802, before handing it back to the Batavian Republic, as the Netherlands was then known. However, the Batavian administration was short-lived, because Britain decided to reoccupy the Cape in January 1806 due to its strategic position and thereafter administered it as a crown colony.

Many burghers of the Cape Colony struggled to adjust to British rule: colonial governors were unsympathetic towards the Dutch language and stood idly by during stock theft by Xhosa groups on the colony's eastern border. The burghers also

President MT Steyn.

felt they weren't compensated well enough when their slaves were freed, in 1834.

Their dissatisfaction was to lead to the Great Trek in 1838, when significant numbers of the chiefly Dutch-speaking population began to leave the Cape in search of a better and independent life in the interior. These disaffected Voortrekkers would later go on to form the Republic of the Orange Free State and the South African Republic, or Transvaal.

The region between the Vaal and Orange rivers in central, present-day South Africa came under British rule in 1848. Major Henry Warden – illegitimate grandson of Bonnie Prince Charlie, the pretender to the British throne – was appointed British Resident of the new Orange River Sovereignty. Basotho, Griqua, Barolong and Koranna people, as well as Boers, constituted the Sovereignty's diverse people; territorial disputes and stock theft triggered frequent conflicts. Despite Warden's efforts to preserve law and order, continuing discord saw military action against King Moshoeshoe's Basotho people. Defeated, along with their allies, in battles at Viervoet (1851) and Berea (1852), the British eventually withdrew from the Sovereignty in 1854.

On 23 February 1854, the signing of the Bloemfontein Convention brought the Republic of the Orange Free State into being. Its rulers – an elected Volksraad (parliament) and a state president with executive and administrative authority – inherited not only empty state coffers but also persistent conflict with the Basotho, who continued to stake their claim to land whose borders the British had long since demarcated. In addition, livestock theft led to regular conflict.

The new state's economic development lagged as a result, a lag that persisted through the terms

The flag of the Republic of the Orange Free State was first raised at Fort Bloemfontein in 1856. When British troops occupied Bloemfontein on 13 March 1900, during the Anglo-Boer War, soldiers removed several flags from public buildings. This specific flag was removed from the city hall by Second Lieutenant GV Clowes.

of office of presidents Josias Philippus Hoffman (1854–1855), Jacobus Nicolaas Boshof (1855–1859) and Marthinus Wessel Pretorius (1859–1863). Thanks to the effective commando system, the Free State was able to sustain itself.

It was only during the term of lawyer and statesman Johannes Henricus (Jan) Brand (1864–1888) that the republic began to gain purchase. From 1867, rich diamond deposits were discovered in the Kimberley region. This region, which also contained 143 farms, was Orange Free State territory. However, Nicolaas Waterboer, the Griqua captain, laid claim to it, petitioning for it to be placed under British rule. Sir Henry Barkly, the British high commissioner, acted as mediator and allowed Waterboer's claim, whereafter the region was incorporated into the Cape Colony.

In 1876, a Cape court upheld the Orange Free State's claim and ruled that Britain was to compensate the Free State to the value of £90 000. Brand used this money to found a national bank and establish rail infrastructure in the Orange Free State. In addition, his attempts to solve the Basotholand dispute through military action in the Third Basotho War (1867–1868) succeeded.

With a constitution based on the models of France and the United States and an efficient bureaucracy – many of whose members hailed from Scotland – the Orange Free State was soon known as a model republic. It blossomed economically as new markets for its agricultural products opened up in Kimberley and the Transvaal, where gold was discovered in the 1880s. The building of the railway, by which an increasing range of products arrived in and left the republic, promised even greater prosperity.

Francis William Reitz (1889–1895) and Marthinus Theunis (MT) Steyn (1896–1902) succeeded Brand as president. The republic's governance was evident in its effective civil service, high-quality education and capital city graced with imposing structures, such as the Presidency, the Government Building and the Fourth Raadsaal.

Marthinus Theunis (MT) Steyn was elected president of the Orange Free State on 19 February 1896. He used this gold pen to sign his name upon being sworn in at the Tweetoringkerk, then the main church in Bloemfontein.

A rosette containing the crest of the South African Republic set against a background in the colours of the republican flags. It signifies the republics' solidarity in the face of war.

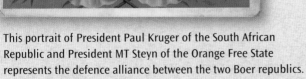

This portrait of President Paul Kruger of the South African Republic and President MT Steyn of the Orange Free State represents the defence alliance between the two Boer republics.

The South African Republic

Great Britain recognised the South African Republic, or Transvaal, as an independent state at the signing of the Sand River Convention on 17 January 1852. The new state's constitution made provision for an elected Volksraad (legislative authority), a president (executive authority) and a judicial authority, as well as a citizen force in the form of a commando system.

Marthinus Wessel Pretorius was elected Commandant General in 1853. In January 1857, he was sworn in as the South African Republic's first state president. Thomas Francois Burgers succeeded him in 1872. Significant economic, political and diplomatic challenges characterised these terms of office, diluting the young state's powers. Conflict with indigenous groups within the state's borders persisted. At the same time, the South African Republic needed to maintain strong diplomatic relations with Great Britain,

Paul Kruger was the South African Republic's third state president.

A crest of the Transvaal Volunteer Units showing the South African Republic coat of arms, which appeared on postage stamps, banknotes, official correspondence, coins and buildings, among others. Other symbols of the state included the Vierkleur flag, a state coat of arms and the anthem 'Kent gij dat Volk'.

which, time and again, impeded its attempts to gain independent access to a port.

Lord Carnarvon, the British secretary of state for colonies, used the South African Republic's weak financial position, its inability to control the indigenous groups within its borders and its diplomatic problems as an excuse to put into action a plan for federation with Britain. He dispatched Sir Theophilus Shepstone, Natal's secretary for native affairs, with a small force to the South African Republic, which Britain annexed on 12 April 1877.

The Transvalers responded, initially, to what the Volksraad considered to be an unlawful act with a policy of passive resistance. Paul Kruger's two fruitless visits to London indicated just how determined Britain was not to back down from the annexation.

With emotions running high, disgruntled Transvalers transferred power, in 1880, to the triumvirate of Paul Kruger, Piet Joubert and Marthinus Wessel Pretorius. An incident of civil disobedience at Potchefstroom, discussed in the next section, sparked the outbreak of the First War of Independence (or First Anglo-Boer War). From December 1880 to February 1881, the British were defeated in a series of battles – including those at Bronkhorstspruit and Majuba.

Peace talks followed, although the South African Republic was to win back its independence only in part at the Pretoria Convention in August 1881. The Convention granted full self-determination of internal affairs, but forbade any agreements with foreign powers (barring the Republic of the Orange Free State) without British approval.

With Paul Kruger's election in 1883, a new era dawned for the South African Republic. Kruger's decisive military and political leadership during the First Anglo-Boer War had endeared him to the Transvaal burghers. In 1884, he forged a new agreement with Great Britain; called the London Convention, it granted the South African Republic greater diplomatic independence.

With economic growth as its aim, the state improved its education system and struck out to link Pretoria by rail to Delagoa Bay at Lourenço Marques (now Maputo) in Portuguese East Africa, a move that would make the South African Republic independent of British-controlled South African ports.

In 1886, the South African Republic's fortunes changed dramatically. The discovery of abundant gold deposits on the Witwatersrand was a turning point for the young state, which blossomed economically and all but forgot its once-precarious existence. But this, too, had a cost: the state's newfound mineral wealth drew renewed attention from Britain and an influx of foreigners, christened 'Uitlanders'.

It was not long before some Uitlander leaders claimed suffrage for the newcomers they represented. Over time, the Uitlander question fanned the nascent flames of conflict between the South African Republic and Britain.

ZAR coinage

A gold pound from the South African Republic, 1898, showing the coat of arms. Paul Kruger appears on the reverse. The first South African Republic coins were minted in 1892. In 1898 Kruger laid the cornerstone of the National Bank and Mint building on Pretoria's Church Square. 🔫

The First War of Independence

Great Britain's recognition of the independence of the South African Republic (Transvaal) in 1852 did not prevent it from annexing the republic on 12 April 1877: under Lord Carnarvon, British aspirations saw South Africa's colonies and states harnessed into a British federation.

Paul Kruger and other Transvaal government representatives took aim at the annexation through petitions and protest meetings, but to no avail. Tensions built as patriotism ran high; at the end of 1880, opposition spilled over into armed resistance at Potchefstroom, and Transvalers laid siege to towns where British garrisons were stationed, among them Pretoria, Potchefstroom, Wakkerstroom, Standerton, Lydenburg, Rustenburg and Marabastad outside Pietersburg.

It was South African Republic forces that claimed the first victory, on 20 December 1880, at Bronkhorstspruit. A shocked General George Pomeroy Colley, governor of Natal and British commander in South Africa, referred to the battle, in a letter to his sister, as 'a sort of Isandhlwana on a smaller scale'. Colley formulated a strategy to relieve the besieged British through an advance from Natal; the republic responded by stationing 1 500 Transvalers, under Commandant General Piet Joubert, at Laingsnek near Majuba Hill – the 'hill of doves'.

With his forces defeated in battles at Laingsnek, on 28 January 1881, and Skuinshoogte (Ingogo), on 8 February, Colley decided to occupy Majuba. From this position on the Transvaal's border with Natal, British forces could better observe the Boer positions at Laingsnek.

Ras cannons

The Ras cannon was built by the Ras family during the First Anglo-Boer War. Each barrel was made of eight wrought-iron wagon-wheel hoops. 'Martienie', the first cannon, fired 59 shots at the British fort at Rustenburg on 8 January 1881. The cannons were moved to Pretoria after the war, where they served as signal guns. The manufacture of these guns is regarded as the beginning of the arms industry in South Africa.

On the morning of 27 February, Hendrina Joubert – Commandant General Joubert's wife, who always accompanied him to battle – recorded the first sighting of 'Rooibaadjies' (red jackets) on Majuba Hill. (During the First War of Independence, British soldiers wore red jackets, which made them easy to spot; during the Anglo-Boer War, the British wore khaki uniforms.)

Joubert ordered his forces to storm the Kop, as the hill was known, before the British had the chance to dig in and haul their artillery up the hill. Under British fire, the Transvalers stormed the hilltop, conquering it after an intense battle that took Colley's life.

Boer casualties numbered five wounded and one dead, with one of the wounded succumbing weeks later. British losses were significantly higher: of 284 casualties, 96 men lost their lives. The Boer victory marked a provisional end to Britain's federal aspirations in South Africa.

The Orange Free State's president Jan Brand helped to negotiate a ceasefire, with peace being officially concluded on 21 March 1881. The Transvaal regained only partial independence at the Pretoria Convention of 3 August 1881, however, with Britain forbidding any agreements between the Transvaal and other foreign powers.

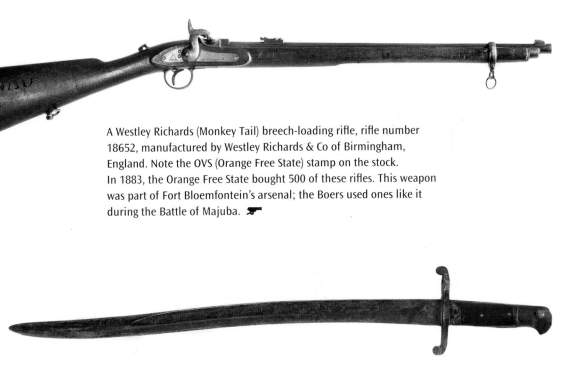

A Westley Richards (Monkey Tail) breech-loading rifle, rifle number 18652, manufactured by Westley Richards & Co of Birmingham, England. Note the OVS (Orange Free State) stamp on the stock. In 1883, the Orange Free State bought 500 of these rifles. This weapon was part of Fort Bloemfontein's arsenal; the Boers used ones like it during the Battle of Majuba.

A sword bayonet taken from a fallen British officer by Field Cornet WJ Goosen during the Battle of Majuba.

The Jameson Raid, 1895–1896

South Africa's two independent Boer republics – in particular the South African Republic (Transvaal) – had long been a thorn in the side of British prime minister Lord Salisbury and his secretary of state for colonies, Joseph Chamberlain. Having two Boer republics in the interior was inconsistent with Britain's vision of expanding its colonial empire in southern Africa.

In 1886, rich gold reserves were discovered on the Witwatersrand, beginning a dramatic economic transformation of the South African Republic. Holding the Transvaal close within its sphere of influence, Britain surmised, would prevent other colonial powers from appropriating the republic and its vast mineral wealth.

On 29 December 1895 – with Chamberlain's knowledge and tacit approval – Dr Leander Starr Jameson, a British citizen, attempted a coup to wrest the South African Republic from Paul Kruger. The driving force behind the raid was Cecil John Rhodes, prime minister of the Cape Colony, and his dreams of a unified British Empire from the Cape to Cairo.

The Reform Committee was established in the run-up to the coup, a group of 64 men who shared a British inclination – including a number of wealthy mine bosses, or Randlords, as they were known. Their plan was to trigger an armed uprising in Johannesburg and, with Dr Jameson's help, overthrow the Kruger government. Whereas the urban uprising failed because of a lack of interest, Jameson resolved to see his plans through.

With 365 men from the British South African Police, 113 from the Bechuanaland Border Police, a handful of volunteers and 11 pieces of artillery, Jameson crossed the Transvaal border from Bechuanaland (present-day Botswana). It did not take long for the Kruger government to get wind of the incursion: the invaders neglected to cut some of the republic's telegraph lines.

In retaliation, the government deployed 1 500 western Transvaal burghers from several commandos, under General Piet Cronjé. The two forces clashed at Doornkop, near Krugersdorp, on Vlakfontein farm, on 2 January 1896.

After heavy fighting, Jameson and his men surrendered.

The British government was obliged to condemn the invasion, and Rhodes was duty-bound to step down as Cape premier. Kruger embarrassed the British government further by handing Jameson and his officers over to be tried in Britain.

In the wake of the raid, great diplomatic tension arose between Britain and the South African Republic. Another consequence was a renewed defence alliance between the South African Republic and Orange Free State – one that was to lead to large-scale militarisation by the two Boer republics.

Dr Leander Starr Jameson was a doctor and politician. At the time of the raid, he was also the administrator of the British South African (Chartered) Company in Mashonaland, in present-day Zimbabwe. *Western Cape Archives*

To end the fighting on
2 January 1896, Jameson
and his men signalled their
surrender by tying the
Vlakfontein housekeeper's
white apron to a whipstock.
With Jameson exhausted and
bewildered, Sir John Willoughby,
one of his officers, took the lead
in composing their letter of
surrender. This inkpot (left)
was on the writing desk at which
the letter was written.

A Boer commando enters Johannesburg after the Jameson Raid. Relations between
the South African Republic and British Empire soured dramatically after the raid.

BOER COMMANDO.

The Bloemfontein Conference

The discovery of gold on the Witwatersrand attracted an influx of foreigners, termed 'Uitlanders', to the South African Republic (Transvaal). Paul Kruger's government had misgivings about these newcomers' loyalty to the Transvaal – especially those from Britain. The South African Republic could ill afford the furthering of British imperialist interests. In 1890, as a countermeasure, Kruger increased the residence period for citizenship from seven to 14 years.

In 1897, on the eve of the war, Sir Alfred Milner was appointed British high commissioner to South Africa. His imperialist mandate made him highly intolerant of the South African Republic and, with Joseph Chamberlain, British secretary of state for colonies, he seized upon foreigners' voting rights as an excuse to draw the republic into the British Empire.

Using the so-called Uitlander question, Milner applied increasing pressure on the South African Republic until, a handful of months before the war, Orange Free State president MT Steyn managed to bring Kruger and Milner together at a conference in Bloemfontein.

The conference, held from 31 May to 5 June 1899 in the newly built Railway Bureau building, sought a peaceful resolution to the tensions around the Uitlander franchise question.

Kruger declared his willingness to restore the seven-year residence period for citizenship. Milner dismissed the concession out of hand, countering with a five-year period, which Kruger rejected. Milner accused Kruger of running the South African Republic as if it were a farm, treating those who came to live in it as tenants, to which Kruger responded by saying, 'These strangers come to me to get rich, and now they want to fight about farm ownership rights too.'

The conference ended in a stalemate – an outcome which, it later emerged through correspondence, Milner and Chamberlain had set out to provoke. On 5 June, Milner declared: 'The Conference is absolutely at an end, and there is no obligation on either side arising out of it. The Bloemfontein Conference made retreat for ever impossible.'

Transvaal attorney general Jan Smuts echoed this by declaring: 'It is perfectly clear that Milner is planning to make war.'

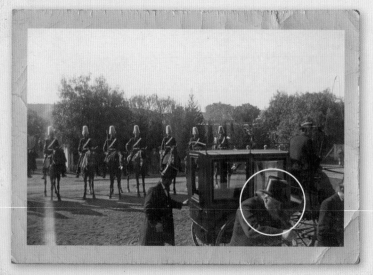

President Paul Kruger (circled) on the steps of the Railway Bureau building during the Bloemfontein Conference.

The Bloemfontein Conference took place around this table from 31 May to 5 June 1899. The full oak set consisted of a conference table with 14 chairs, a bookcase, two sofas and two smaller desks with chairs. ↗

Sir Alfred Milner.

Members of the public in front of the newly completed Railway Bureau building at the time of the Bloemfontein Conference.

An Ultimatum, and
the Outbreak of War

The failure of the Bloemfontein Conference made war unavoidable. Preparations began on both sides: the British government bolstered its forces in South Africa, and the Boer republics ordered arms from Europe. This did not prevent further attempts to break the deadlock over Uitlander rights, however; new conditions for settlement were put to Britain, and, ultimately, the South African Republic agreed to give Uitlanders the vote after five years of residence.

The goalposts had shifted, however, with the British government putting forward new conditions that sought to hobble the Transvaal's independence. It became clear that the British government had no further interest in a peaceful settlement. Continued negotiations would be futile.

The government of the South African Republic, assisted by the Orange Free State, drafted an ultimatum, which was handed over to Britain's representative in Pretoria, Sir William Conyngham Greene, on Monday 9 October 1899.

The ultimatum's critical requirements were as follows:

• *That all points of mutual difference shall be regulated by the friendly course of arbitration or by whatever amicable way may be agreed upon by this Government with Her Majesty's Government.*

....

• *That the troops on the borders of this Republic shall be instantly withdrawn.*

....

• *That all reinforcements of troops which have arrived in South Africa since June 1st, 1899, shall be removed from South Africa within a reasonable time, to be agreed upon with this Government, and with a mutual assurance and guarantee upon the part of this Government that no attack upon or hostilities against any portion of the possessions*

Queen Victoria, British monarch from 1837 to 1901. Her portrait graced the front rooms of countless homes in the two republics: many Afrikaner families were convinced that her government had misled her about the war's true cause, and Free Staters and Transvalers liked to refer to their compatriots in the Cape Colony as 'Queen Victoria's Afrikaners'.

of the British Government shall be made by the Republic during further negotiations within a period of time to be subsequently agreed upon between the Governments, and this Government will, on compliance therewith, be prepared to withdraw the armed burghers of this Republic from the borders.

....

• That Her Majesty's troops which are now on the high seas shall not be landed in any part of South Africa.

....

• This Government must press for an immediate and affirmative answer to these four questions, and earnestly requests Her Majesty's Government to return such an answer before or upon Wednesday, October 11th, 1899, not later than five o'clock p.m., and it desires further to add that, in the event of unexpectedly no satisfactory answer being received by it within that interval, it will with great regret be compelled to regard the action of Her Majesty's Government as a formal declaration of war, and will not hold itself responsible for the consequences thereof, and that in the event of any further movements of troops taking place within the above-mentioned time in the nearer directions of our borders, the Government will be compelled to regard that also as a formal declaration of war.

A coded telegram from President Paul Kruger to President MT Steyn about the ultimatum.

The republics prepared their commandos in anticipation, while Chamberlain convinced the British cabinet to prepare an ultimatum of its own. With these words, the British government rejected the Boer republics' ultimatum: 'Her Majesty's Government have received with great regret the peremptory demands of the Government of the South African Republic. You will inform the Government of the South African Republic, in Reply that the conditions demanded by the South African Republic are of such as Her Majesty's Government deem it impossible to discuss.'

Two days later, on 11 October 1899, the Anglo-Boer War – also known as the Second War of Independence, the Transvaal War or the South African War – broke out.

The Siege of Ladysmith. A Long Tom 155-mm gun fires on the town in this painting by German artist Sylvester Reisacher.

CHAPTER 2

Initial Battles and Sieges

Kraaipan, 12 October 1899

The South African Republic's campaign strategy included securing the Transvaal's western border by ruling out Colonel Robert Baden-Powell's small British garrison stationed at Mafeking, in Bechuanaland (now Botswana). General Koos de la Rey and his 800-strong Lichtenburg commando were summoned to attack a British force, numbering 1 000 men, that had gathered near Moshettestat. They were also tasked with disabling the region's telegraph lines and railways.

Finding no trace of the British force, De la Rey, with the Lichtenburg, Potchefstroom and Klerksdorp commandos, pushed on to Kraaipan, a railway siding between Vryburg and Mafeking, which they reached on 12 October 1899. Meanwhile, Baden-Powell had dispatched a train to Vryburg to collect munitions, including two pieces of artillery, to use against the Boers. An armoured locomotive – the HMT (Her Majesty's Train) *Mosquito* – accompanied the train.

On its way back, the locomotive derailed at Kraaipan on 12 October at about 10.45 pm due to sabotage by the Boers. The *Mosquito*'s commander, Lieutenant RH Nesbitt, ordered the repair of the damaged rails, but the commotion had roused the sleeping Boers, who were camped nearby. They quickly took up positions around the siding.

Field Cornet Coetzee fired the first shot of the Anglo-Boer War at 10.45 pm. In its wake, heavy fire from the rest of the commando drove the British to shelter inside the *Mosquito*; they returned rifle and light artillery fire. All hopes of escape were dashed, however, when a shot from one of the Boers' four pieces of artillery disabled the *Mosquito*'s boiler. Nesbitt was also wounded in the skirmish.

It was not long before the British surrendered and the Boers plundered two ageing mountain guns and some caches of ammunition, bringing the first engagement of the war to a close.

Boers in front of HMT *Mosquito*. The point where the steam engine was hit by artillery has been circled.

A cup fashioned from the shell casing of the first round fired at Kraaipan. It was given as a gift to General Christiaan de Wet, who later gave it to one Lieutenant AP Troskie.

'Armoured trains had been secretly constructed in the railway works, and one of these, the *Mosquito*, under Lt Nesbitt was sent down to Vryburg to fetch a couple of 5-inch howitzers that Baden-Powell hoped to get sent up from Cape Town. All that Cape Town had to offer were two antiquated muzzle-loading 7-pounders, that had been fished up out of the recess of the ordnance stores.'
– *The Times History of the War in South Africa 1899–1902*

A list of equipment that was on board HMT *Mosquito* when it was intercepted by the Boers.

The Battle of Talana Hill, 20 October 1899

When war broke out, the republican forces resolved to capture Natal, a British colony, as soon as possible. The majority of the 24 000-strong Transvaal and Free State forces invaded northern Natal in the first few days of the war, with Dundee as their immediate goal. Dundee housed a substantial British garrison, under the command of Major General Sir William Penn Symons. In addition, General George White commanded the garrison at Ladysmith, numbering some 9 000 men, as well as a Naval Brigade and 36 guns of varying calibres.

To secure a view of Penn Symons's camp, Boer general Lucas Meyer ordered his 1 500-man force and three artillery pieces to take up positions atop Talana Hill, Lennox Hill and Smith's Nek. Meyer's words, *'maak maar los, ou seun'* (let rip, my boy), unleashed the Boer bombardment on the British camp. Not all of the Boer grapeshot rounds detonated in the soft ground, but this did

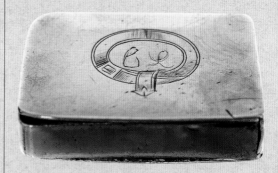

A British soldier's snuff box, found on the Talana battlefield by a Boer fighter.

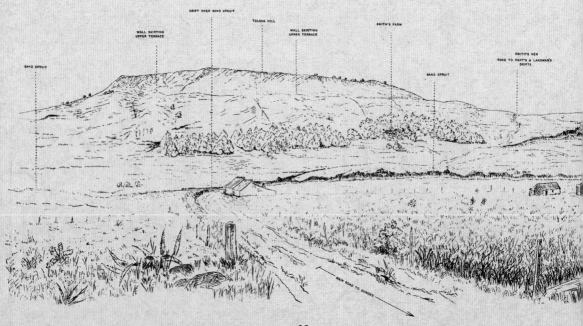

TALANA HILL, LOOKING EAST.
FROM AN UNFINISHED DRAWING BY THE LATE CAPTAIN W. C. C. ERSKINE, R.N.I.
COMPLETED BY CAPTAIN K. M. DAVIE, GLOUCESTER REGIMENT

not prevent the bombardment from sowing chaos in the British camp.

Penn Symons ordered a counterattack on the Boers' strategic positions on Talana Hill. British artillerymen dug in on the hill and launched such an effective bombardment that the Boers and their artillery had to fall back. British infantry, led by the Royal Dublin Fusiliers, moved forward.

The British had occupied a farmstead at the foot of Talana Hill. Its sturdy, stone-walled outbuildings were surrounded by a stand of blue gum trees. However, the British were pinned down by Boer fire from Talana and Lennox hills. Penn Symons, who had decided to lead the charge, was mortally wounded. The British soldiers, now under Major General JH Yule's command, continued with the charge, despite coming under heavy Mauser fire from the Boers.

With British cavalry moving behind the firing line, the Boers on Talana Hill feared being surrounded and began a gradual withdrawal. British pressure on Boer positions increased steadily, and a series of British infantry charges followed the force's heavy artillery bombardment. In the dying moments of the battle, Danie Theron's Reconnaissance Corps and Colonel John Blake's Irish Volunteers, who fought on the side of the Boers, managed to trap a group of 243 British cavalrymen in a cattle kraal on a nearby farm. In the end, the British forces gained the upper hand. However, they neglected to follow up on their victory.

The Battle of Talana was the Anglo-Boer War's first major battle in Natal, and the first to claim the life of a senior British officer. In its aftermath, British forces fell back on Ladysmith and the Boers occupied Dundee soon afterwards.

The Talana battlefield, showing the hills from which the Boers bombarded the British.

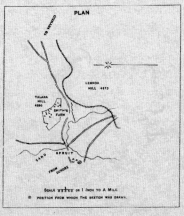

A plan of Talana sketched by KM Davie of the Gloucestershire Regiment, with help from a map of the area put together by Captain William Douglas Erskine.

Elandslaagte, 21 October 1899

On 19 October 1899, one Field Cornet Pienaar intercepted a British supply train at Elandslaagte station, northeast of Ladysmith. News of the captured train reached General Michiel Kock and his Johannesburg commando, which was accompanied by the Dutch and German corps.

The events that followed can likely be attributed to one man's ambition, or to greed: despite the order from Commandant General Piet Joubert, commander in chief of the Transvaal and Orange Free State forces in Natal, that Transvaal forces should stand down until the Free State contingent joined them, Kock went ahead and occupied Elandslaagte.

Enthralled by the spoils from the enemy supply train, Kock's men did not even realise that they were under attack until the British shells started exploding in their midst. Thanks to intelligence obtained from some prisoners of war who had escaped from the Boers, the British commander,

General John French, knew exactly how much resistance he would face from Kock's commando. The latter took up positions on higher ground around the station, driving the British back with artillery fire. Convinced that he had defeated the British, Kock went back to plundering the train. Little did he know that French had only fallen back to wait for reinforcements.

On the arrival of the Royal Field Artillery, with its 2 500 men and multiple field guns, French could, after something of an intermission, resume his attack on Boer positions to retake Elandslaagte. Heavy frontal and flank attacks followed the bombardment of Boer positions. It was only when the battle intensified that Kock realised he was in a dire situation, and pinned his hopes on reinforcements led by Commandant Adolf Schiel's German corps. Kock had sent Schiel west to take up positions on the Biggarsberg, but Schiel's men were now cut off from Kock. The German fighters launched a frontal assault to try to drive the British back.

Field Cornet Pienaar (circled) and his men at the train they plundered at Elandslaagte.

The heavens opened. Heavy rain concealed the advancing British infantrymen; charge after charge threw Boer defences into chaos, with the British in close pursuit. With cries of 'Revenge Majuba!', the lances and swords of the 5th Dragoon Guards and 5th (Royal Irish) Lancers sowed death among the fleeing Boers, who saw in the British lances echoes of the weapons they had faced in conflicts with indigenous groups. Kock himself was critically injured, succumbing later to his wounds.

Of Schiel's commando, several were wounded or killed. The rest, including Schiel himself, were captured and held as prisoners of war. Among the Boer fallen were Count Harra von Zeppelin, nephew of the famous German airship pioneer, and Dr Herman Coster, former Transvaal attorney general and a member of the Dutch corps.

The annals record Elandslaagte as a great victory for the British, one for which four Victoria Crosses were awarded.

A cavalryman of the 5th (Royal Irish) Lancers recalled the battle at Elandslaagte as follows: 'We got a charge at them; they asked for mercy, but we were told not to give them any, and I assure you they got none. We went along sticking our lances through them – it was a terrible thing, but you have to do it in a case like this.'
– *Vir vryheid en reg: Anglo-Boereoorlog-gedenkboek*

A lance of the type used by the 5th (Royal Irish) Lancers. Burgher Adriaan JF Prinsloo took this from a British lancer during the battle.

Insignia of the 5th (Royal Irish) Lancers.

The Siege of Mafeking, 13 October 1899–17 May 1900

Photos and travellers' accounts describe the Mafeking of 1899 as a small town of tin-roofed houses set in an arid, sandy landscape. Its 1 700 white and 7 500 Barolong souls sustained a Standard Bank, a few shops and smaller businesses, and Bradley's Hotel; the Barolong settlement was on the outskirts of the town.

Mafeking's small size belied the town's strategic importance, situated, as it was, on the rail line between the Cape and Bulawayo in southern Rhodesia (now Zimbabwe). Shortly before the war, Colonel Robert Baden-Powell – commander of the British garrison at Mafeking – stockpiled provisions and fortified the town in anticipation of a siege.

Baden-Powell's force of about 716 comprised 469 men of the Protectorate Regiment, 83 from the Bechuanaland Rifles – both from Bechuanaland (now Botswana) – 72 from the British South African Police and 92 from the

Sol Plaatje (circled) at the hearing of a Barolong man, in which he acted as court interpreter. Lord Edward Cecil (at the table) heard the case. *Western Cape Archives*

Cape Police. He had also gathered a 300-man Town Guard and recruited 300 Tshidi-Barolongs, whom he armed. This was in contravention of the tacit agreement between both warring parties not to arm the black population.

Sol Plaatje

The newspaper editor, politician and author Sol Plaatje is one of the few black South Africans to have written down their Anglo-Boer War experiences. During the siege of Mafeking, Plaatje worked as a court interpreter for the British authorities. He kept a diary that was published about 70 years later, in 1972, as *The Boer War Diary of Sol T. Plaatje*.

Plaatje was a leading figure in the black community and also the first secretary-general of the South African National Congress, which was established in Bloemfontein in 1912 and later became the African National Congress (ANC). In his best-known work, *Native Life in South Africa*, Plaatje strongly criticised the Natives' Land Act of 1913, which severely limited land ownership by black South Africans.

Extracts from Lady Sarah Wilson's diary:
'At that date (11th of October 1899) the Mafeking garrison consisted of about seven or eight hundred trained troops. The artillery, under Major Panzera, comprised four old muzzle-loading seven-pounder guns with a short range, a one-pound Hotchkiss, one Nordenfelt, and about seven .303 Maxims – in fact no large modern pieces whatever. The town guard, hastily enrolled, amounted to 441 defenders, among whom nationalities were curiously mixed. This force did not appear sufficiently strong to resist three or four thousand Boers with field-guns … but everyone remained wonderfully calm, and the townspeople rose to the occasion in a most creditable manner.'
– *South African Memories: Social, Warlike and Sporting – From Diaries Written at the Time*

A ten-shilling Mafeking Siege note, no 2615, showing the watermark of the Croxley writing paper on which it was printed. The notes were printed from February to March 1900 by Townsend & Son, a printer in the besieged town.

ABOVE Colonel Robert Baden-Powell sketching on his veranda during the siege.
RIGHT British soldiers hand out rations to residents of the Barolong township at Mafeking. *Western Cape Archives*

His artillery comprised seven .303 Maxim machine guns and seven artillery pieces, most of which were ageing. Mafeking's defenders made up for this artillery shortage by repairing the barrel of the Lord Nelson, an old ship's cannon that was being used as a gatepost, and using it to fire dynamite grenades at Boer positions. In addition, they fashioned a steel pipe into a makeshift cannon, and christened it 'The Wolf'.

The Boers, having already destroyed the town's telegraph and rail links, besieged Mafeking on

The inscription on this Sheffield silver cigarette holder reads: 'From Luwanika chief of Barotsiland to DH'. The owner of the cigarette holder was a member of the Protectorate Regiment during the siege of Mafeking.

13 October 1899. Shortly afterwards, Captain Lord Charles Cavendish-Bentinck's reconnaissance patrol skirmished with part of the 5 600-strong Boer force under General Piet Cronjé; the patrol had to flee, tail between its legs, back to Mafeking.

Cronjé's forces comprised, mainly, commandos from Rustenburg, Marico, Wolmaransstad, Lichtenburg and Bloemhof. Their primary ordnance was a Long Tom 155-mm gun from Fort Daspoort, in Pretoria; smaller ordnance included guns that had been captured in the Jameson Raid, operated by artillerymen of the Transvaal State Artillery.

The siege of Mafeking would run for 216 days, until 17 May 1900. Supplies diminished rapidly; in addition to food shortages, the interruption of normal trade compelled Baden-Powell to print a special currency unit, the Mafeking Siege banknote. When the town's postage stamps ran out, special Mafeking Siege stamps were produced. Barolong messengers smuggled post out of the town.

Martial law punished offences such as food theft in draconian fashion – in one instance, Sol Plaatje, who would become one of the founders of the African National Congress, acted as an interpreter in the trial of a Barolong man who had stolen a goat. The man was sentenced to death.

Baden-Powell armed increasing numbers of Barolong and Fingo defenders. Known to

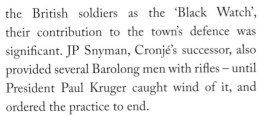

One of the Boer positions on the outskirts of Mafeking.

The Gaelic Saloon in Mafeking after it was hit by Boer artillery. *Western Cape Archives*

the British soldiers as the 'Black Watch', their contribution to the town's defence was significant. JP Snyman, Cronjé's successor, also provided several Barolong men with rifles – until President Paul Kruger caught wind of it, and ordered the practice to end.

While the British media reported widely about all the three of the besieged towns – Mafeking, Ladysmith and Kimberley – Mafeking was a media favourite. The *Daily Mail* appointed Lady Sarah Wilson, one of future prime minister Winston Churchill's aunts – as correspondent. (Edward Cecil, son of British prime minister Lord Salisbury, was another British aristocrat caught in the siege.) The *Mafeking Mail*, a special newspaper, also made an appearance during the siege.

Periodic bombardments – from the Long Tom gun in particular – characterised the siege. Despite these, and a few uncoordinated attacks, the Boers never did succeed in capturing Mafeking. The tide of war turned in favour of the British, especially after the capture of Bloemfontein, obliging the Boer war council to lift the siege.

Colonel Bryan Mahon's 2 500-man relief column rode into Mafeking on 17 May 1900. The news of the relief of Mafeking was received with great jubilation throughout the British Empire; in London, thousands gathered in Piccadilly Circus in celebration.

A special supplement in the *Natal Mercury* about the relief of Mafeking. In the centre is a portrait of Robert Baden-Powell, commander of British forces in the besieged town.

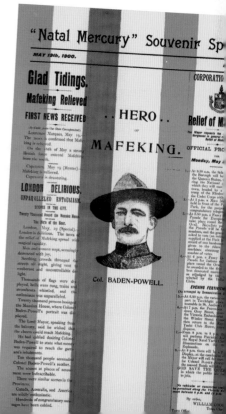

The Siege of Kimberley, 15 October 1899–15 February 1900

Born from the discovery of diamonds in 1867, the town of Kimberley soon flourished, with over 50 000 people flocking here within a year. By 1882, the town could boast the first electric streetlights in the southern hemisphere.

Named for British colonial secretary Lord John Wodehouse, 1st Earl of Kimberley, it was the northern Cape Colony's largest town and the headquarters of Cecil John Rhodes' De Beers diamond company.

The British may have compensated the Orange Free State for the loss of the diamond fields, which were finally annexed to the Cape in 1880, but the Boers had long felt that the acquisition had not been fair and that the region still belonged to the Orange Free State. It goes without saying, then, that Kimberley, a mere eight kilometres from the Orange Free State's western border, was firmly in the republic's wartime sights.

When war broke out, the Orange Free State war council knew full well that, by assimilating Kimberley and its 13 000 white and 37 000 black inhabitants, it could drum up support for the republican cause among Afrikaners in the Cape Colony. In 1898, the government had even ordered the map of the borders around Kimberley to be redrawn.

The British began preparing for a siege in early September 1899, sending ammunition and food supplies to Kimberley and appointing Lieutenant Colonel Robert George Kekewich – 'Kokewiets' to the Boers – as commander.

At the outbreak of hostilities, the British garrison of 4 219 men, including a Town Guard, had 14 artillery pieces and 11 Maxim machine guns at its disposal. Under the supervision of the Royal Engineers, the town was fortified with sconces and forts, built largely by black mineworkers.

The Orange Free State siege force was 4 800 strong, with Chief Commandant Cornelis Janse Wessels at its head. It had disrupted all rail and telegraph connections on its way to Kimberley; General Koos de la Rey's 2 200-man force soon joined Wessels' men.

Rhodes himself was trapped in the besieged town, together with 45 000 others. De Beers company contributed by making labour, equipment such as searchlights, and tinned foods available to the town.

The De Beers workshops were placed at Kekewich's disposal for the manufacture of artillery projectiles. American engineer George Labram assisted with this, and designed a cannon that was manufactured in the same facility. Called the 'Long Cecil', it fired its first salvo on Boer positions – almost nine kilometres away – on 21 January 1900.

Martial law was proclaimed, limiting business hours in bars and canteens, and imposing a citizen curfew. In January 1900, Kekewich ordered all horses and mules to be placed under military control to supplement the town's food supplies, and a soup kitchen to be established where the unfortunate animals' meat would be prepared.

A Long Tom gun reached the Boers in early February 1900. It fired its first shots on 7 February 1900, causing huge consternation among the townspeople of Kimberley, who responded

A Long Cecil projectile, cast in the De Beers workshop and transformed into a trophy.

Long Cecil, operated by the Diamond Fields Artillery, with designer George Labram standing near the wheel. Labram was mortally wounded when a Long Tom projectile struck the Grand Hotel, in which he was preparing for dinner with Cecil John Rhodes.

by carving shelters into old mine dumps. The Cuthberts store, De Beers offices, Grand Hotel and Anglican and Presbyterian churches sustained heavy damage.

Lord Roberts's advancing army gradually unnerved the Boers. On 15 February 1900, after a siege of 123 days, Roberts's vanguard under General John French freed the town.

A brooch made from a fragment of a Boer projectile fired during the Siege of Kimberley. Townspeople avidly collected these fragments as siege mementos.

Roberts's forces on their way to relieve Kimberley.

'Mention must be made of siege soup – the suggestion of Tim Tyson, then secretary of the Kimberley Club, and as such known by now to nearly half the army. It was prepared at the De Beers Company convict station. To look at, it was a thick grey concoction with lots of vegetables and it was guaranteed free from horse; but I "ha'e me doots". Please remember that by the time you are driven to have recourse to horse he is scraggy, under-fed, and rejected by the remount officer, and there is a general suspicion that he has been slaughtered to prevent death from other causes.' – *War Sketches in Colour*

The Siege of Ladysmith,
2 November 1899–28 February 1900

Most British troops who fought in the war took two months to reach South Africa by ship, which gave the Boer republics an initial advantage and left British forces reluctant to go on the offensive. The British opted to relinquish Dundee to the Boers, despite their victory at Talana, and fell back on Ladysmith. On 30 October 1899, they tried in vain to expel the Boers from Nicholson's Nek and Modderspruit. Demoralised, they referred to this day as 'Mournful Monday', a day that left all telegraph and rail lines destroyed by the Boers.

At a war council meeting on 1 November 1899, Boer leaders resolved to besiege Ladysmith, which would prove to be the final Boer offensive of the Natal campaign. They took up hillside positions at Nicholson's Nek, Umbulwana and Pepworth Hill, gradually surrounding the town.

The damaged Ladysmith city hall shortly after the siege. Used by the 18th Field Hospital, the building was struck by a Long Tom projectile on 30 November 1899, killing 10 patients and a few doctors.

The British launched offensives to dislodge the Boers from these strategic positions, though with scant success. After lodging their artillery pieces – including Long Toms – in the hills around Ladysmith, they began their bombardment of both the town and the British garrison at Caesar Camp.

Before the Boers could surround the town entirely, however, the Naval Brigade managed to move two 4.7-inch guns from HMS *Powerful*, a British cruiser in Durban harbour, to Ladysmith. Christened 'Lady Anne' and 'Bloody Mary', the guns had a range of over nine kilometres – bringing them into direct competition with the Boers' Long Toms.

The warring parties reached an agreement to house all wounded British soldiers in Intombi Camp, outside Ladysmith. This camp would not come under Boer fire.

Surprise attacks launched by both sides had no success to speak of. One such attack, on 8 December 1899, left some Boer artillery pieces, including a Long Tom, damaged on Lombard's Kop. Within the town, morale fell; as food supplies dwindled, British cavalry horses found themselves suited to a different purpose, and dysentery broke out among the troops. Boer bombardments continued unabated, and General Redvers Buller's British forces found themselves checked at every turn in the battles that raged along the Tugela River (now the Thukela). In a bid to raise spirits and give the townspeople something to do, the *Ladysmith Bombshell* and *Ladysmith Lyre* newspapers came into being.

When more British troops eventually made landfall in Durban, republican forces found themselves under ever-increasing pressure. The British breakthrough came at last on 27 February 1900. The 118-day siege was relieved the following day, when the 17th Lancers rode into Ladysmith.

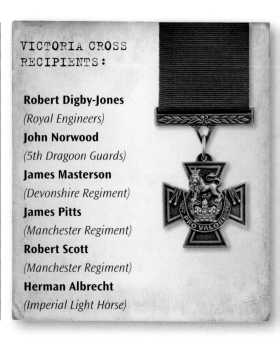

VICTORIA CROSS RECIPIENTS:

Robert Digby-Jones
(Royal Engineers)
John Norwood
(5th Dragoon Guards)
James Masterson
(Devonshire Regiment)
James Pitts
(Manchester Regiment)
Robert Scott
(Manchester Regiment)
Herman Albrecht
(Imperial Light Horse)

Commandant General Piet Joubert (circled) and his staff during the Siege of Ladysmith.

'My force here is terribly reduced in efficiency by disease and there is more enteric and dysentery every day. I have before me our sick report of one month ago. The total sick and wounded then was 436, today the total is 1 578. A month ago, on 1 December, there were 29 cases of enteric fever; today there are 506 besides 285 not yet diagnosed. On 1 December we had only 76 cases of dysentery; today we have 588 cases.'
– Letter from General George White, 4 January 1900, from *The Siege of Ladysmith*

On Christmas Day 1899, the Boers fired two Long Tom salvos over Ladysmith. However, the projectiles that landed in the camp housing the Natal Carbineers and the Imperial Light Horse caused no destruction. Each displayed a message reading, 'With the Compliments of the Season'. The two projectiles were filled with small white bowls like this one, containing Christmas pudding for General White and his men. 🔫

A British troop train arrives at Modder River station in the northern Cape Colony with a Scottish regiment aboard. *Western Cape Archives*

CHAPTER 3

Black Week and the Fall of the Republics

The Battle of Stormberg, 10 December 1899

On 10 December 1899, the British army suffered the first of three devastating defeats in one week at Stormberg, a railway junction near the village of Molteno. Then came defeat at Magersfontein, south of Kimberley, on 11 December, and at Colenso, in Natal, on 15 December. The British press gave the triple misfortune the ominous title of 'Black Week'.

Fearing a British attack from the south, Orange Free State president MT Steyn ordered his commandos to invade the Cape Colony when war broke out, and specifically to seize the strategically important railway junctions at Noupoort, De Aar, Rosmead and Stormberg. The invasion was two-pronged. When reinforcements arrived from the Transvaal, the first group of Orange Free State commandos crossed the Norvalspont bridge on

The Rouxville commando, with General Jan Hendrik Olivier (circled) in the foreground. In the photo, Olivier can be seen wearing the orange sash (see opposite page) made for him by his wife.

A yellow taffeta sash embroidered with the Orange Free State (OVS) crest, which General Jan Olivier wore during the occupation of Aliwal North.

A matchbox belonging to General Olivier, used during the Battle of Stormberg.

General Jan Hendrik Olivier (circled) and members of his commando in January 1900 at the Stormberg railway junction.

1 November and went on to occupy Colesberg two weeks later.

General Jan Hendrik Olivier's second republican force captured the Cape Colony towns of Aliwal North, Venterstad, Burgersdorp, Barkly East and Lady Grey, among others, on 2 November. Chief Commandant Esias Grobler's Orange Free State force had reached the Stormberg region when Olivier also received orders to seize the junction. He sent a small force of about 400 men ahead, and joined them with his remaining 1 750 men and four guns on 7 December. The combined force took up positions in the hills to the south and southwest of the junction.

Two days later, Lieutenant General William Gatacre and his force of 4 500 men arrived at Molteno. Ragged from the train journey and long march, his troops were ordered to prepare for an attack on republican positions. However, Gatacre's scouts were unfamiliar with the region.

Together with a failure to conduct proper reconnaissance, this led to the British running straight into Olivier's positions to the southwest on 10 December. A farmer caught sight of some of Gatacre's vanguard in the early-morning gloom and, mistaking them for stock thieves, opened fire. His shots alerted Boer sentries.

A 400-strong Boer force, under Grobler's command, raced to the scene from a few kilometres west of Olivier's commando. Their attack on Gatacre's force from the rear sowed chaos among the exhausted British troops, who immediately fell back on Molteno. Instead of pursuing the retreating force, Olivier took 672 prisoners of war and two 15-pounder Armstrong guns.

Stormberg proved to many republican-minded Cape Colonists who were considering joining the fray that the mighty British lion could, indeed, be tamed. Many joined the republican forces as Cape rebels.

The Battle of Magersfontein, 11 December 1899

The Battle of Magersfontein was one of the Anglo-Boer War's bloodiest: by late morning on 11 December 1899, the bodies of 288 British and 87 Boer soldiers littered the Magersfontein battlefield.

Magersfontein followed three other engagements in the region, and was part of Lord Methuen's advance on the besieged town of Kimberley in November 1899. At Belmont (23 November) and Graspan (25 November), Methuen succeeded in driving the Boers out of their positions. On 28 November, Methuen faced the combined forces of General Koos de la Rey, General Piet Cronjé and Commandant Jacobus Prinsloo. This third attack took place at Modder River station, about 40 km south of Kimberley. Boer forces were well entrenched,

but British troops posed a threat to their right flank, pushing them to abandon their positions. General De la Rey's son, Adrian (Adaan) de la Rey, was fatally wounded here.

Cronjé's men dug in at Magersfontein on 5 December to check Methuen's advance. Their trenches, ably prepared at the foot of Magersfontein Kop and the surrounding hills, and which stretched over about 23 km, made for strong positions, with the Scandinavian corps installed in a clearing to the east.

It was clear to Methuen's 15 000-strong force that the Boers, once again, had the literal and figurative high ground. So, on a hot, dusty 10 December, Methuen unleashed upon them the heaviest bombardment since the Siege of Sevastopol during the Crimean War (1853–1856).

General Koos de la Rey (circled) and his men at Magersfontein. His son Adriaan (Adaan) was wounded at Modder River and later succumbed to his wounds at Jacobsdal.

ABOVE and BELOW Trenches at Magersfontein about seven months after the battle.

The Highland Brigade suffered the heaviest losses at the Battle of Magersfontein.

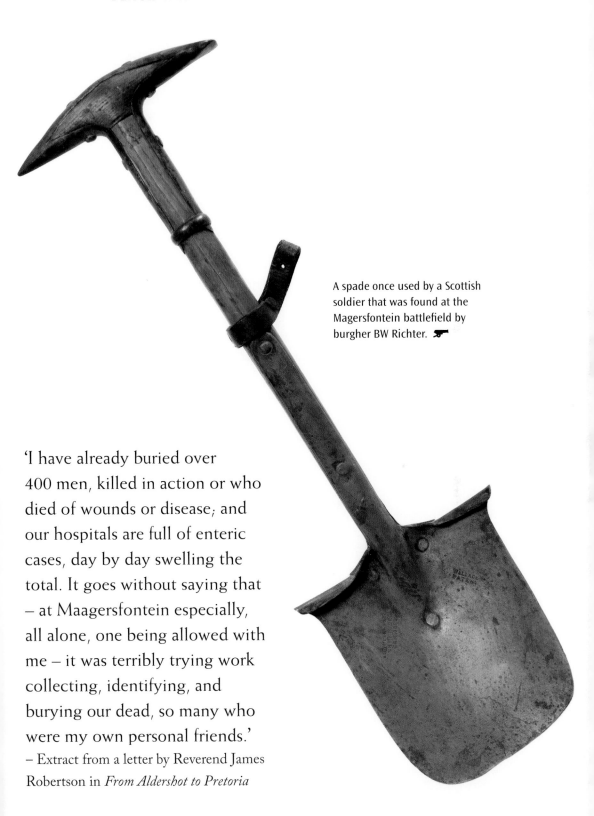

A spade once used by a Scottish soldier that was found at the Magersfontein battlefield by burgher BW Richter.

'I have already buried over 400 men, killed in action or who died of wounds or disease; and our hospitals are full of enteric cases, day by day swelling the total. It goes without saying that – at Maagersfontein especially, all alone, one being allowed with me – it was terribly trying work collecting, identifying, and burying our dead, so many who were my own personal friends.'
– Extract from a letter by Reverend James Robertson in *From Aldershot to Pretoria*

Afrikaans poet JD du Toit (Totius), who would later become a well-known figure, was 22 at the time. That morning, he was reading Psalm 85 to the assembled commando members when Methuen's lyddite shells started tearing into Magersfontein Kop.

The Boers opened fire from the Kop with Martini-Henry rifles, strengthening Methuen's belief that they occupied the high ground. This was all part of the Boers' subterfuge, however: only a handful of Boers were stationed on the Kop, but the clouds of smoke created by the Martini-Henrys made their numbers appear greater.

That night, Methuen began an advance, intent on storming Magersfontein Kop at daybreak. Major General Andrew Wauchope's potent, 3 500-man Highland Brigade accompanied him through difficult terrain and pelting rain that made the night march an ordeal. Oblivious

in the pre-dawn light, they marched, in tight formation, straight into the Boer lines. From their trenches, the Boer forces opened fire.

Hundreds of British troops fled in the chaos. Others were trapped in the battery fire, their close-order formation preventing them from dispersing. It was a slaughter. Methuen's attempts to break through Boer lines failed. The following morning, he had no choice but to fall back to the Modder River.

Over and above the fatalities on the British side – several senior officers, including Wauchope himself, were among the dead – 700 lay wounded and 100 were reported missing. Two Victoria Crosses, seven Distinguished Service Orders and 12 Distinguished Conduct medals were awarded.

On the Boer side, 23 members of the Scandinavian corps were among the dead, with 71 wounded.

In 1890, the then still-unknown artist Frans Oerder emigrated from the Netherlands to the Transvaal and applied for a position within the broader field of the arts. The South African Republic government consequently asked him to paint the telegraph poles along the Delagoa Bay railway line. When war broke out, he was appointed the South African Republic's official war artist. Oerder created several works that depicted commando life, as well as different military positions, such as this sketch, 'Schansen by Magersfontein'.

The Battle of Colenso, 15 December 1899

The Battle of Colenso was the last of Britain's three Black Week defeats. General Redvers Buller, commander of the British forces in South Africa, launched an assault on Boer positions at Colenso, on the Tugela River, on 15 December 1899. Known as 'Rooivers-bul' to the Boers, Buller and his 21 000 men had the relief of Ladysmith, besieged for six weeks, as their primary goal.

General Louis Botha's 3 000 Boer fighters and five guns formed a broad front north of the Tugela River. Botha, the new republican commander on the Tugela line, sought to mislead the British about the strength and distribution of Boer forces by setting up fake ramparts on the other side of the river.

By the time British forces launched their infantry attack at 5.30 am on 15 December, Boer forces at Colenso had already been under heavy artillery fire for two days. Things started to go wrong for the British from the beginning, however, largely due to poor reconnaissance work: they had used an out-of-date map in their preparations.

The map showed a ford in the Tugela River where there was none, placing the British right flank in a dangerous position, unable to cross the river as they had planned. The Boers opened fire with two Long Tom guns, trapping the 5th (Irish) Brigade in a bend in the river and holding their positions despite continued attacks from three directions.

Pressure on British forces increased when two field artillery batteries under Colonel CK Long took up positions too close to the republican firing line. They set up their 12 guns in the positions they had planned, only for accurate rifle fire from the Boer line to put their

British forces used star shells to illuminate the landscape on the banks of the Tugela River at night. *Western Cape Archives*

artillerymen out of action in no time at all. The British countered with three brave attempts, under deadly rifle fire, to retrieve the guns. Lord Roberts's only son, Lieutenant Freddie Roberts, was critically wounded in one of these attempts, succumbing to his wounds the following night. In the end, the British manged to pull only two cannons out of the line of fire – at the expense of many lives. Breaking with century-old British artillery tradition, Buller issued an order to 'abandon the guns'.

An article that appeared in a Pietermaritzburg newspaper on 31 January 1900 quoted Winston Churchill lauding Colonel Long's courage as 'devoted gallantry, urging his gunners to fight their pieces to the last'.

Other British assaults were equally unsuccessful, and at 10 am Buller had no choice but to recall

his troops, earning him the nickname of 'Reverse Buller'. The Boers streamed across the Colenso bridge, plundered ten guns and nine ammunition wagons, and took a number of artillerymen, who had sheltered in ditches, as prisoners of war.

The Battle of Colenso claimed 143 British lives, and left 756 British soldiers wounded and 240 missing. Boer forces lost eight men and reported 30 wounded. The battle revealed Britain's urgent need for a new military strategy in southern Africa.

Black Week rubbed salt into the British wounds of Mafeking, Kimberley and Ladysmith. Britain acknowledged the extent to which it had underestimated the Boers' military capabilities, and abandoned all hopes for a quick victory.

Commandant General Louis Botha, a later prime minister, in the field after the Battle of Colenso. Note the South African Republic coat of arms that appears alongside other engravings on the stock of his Mauser carbine.

British prisoners of war, released by the Boers, march into Pretoria after the city's capture to be rearmed and sent back to the front.

A pendant made of shrapnel from a British grapeshot round. General Botha found the shrapnel in his pocket after the Battle of Colenso on 15 December 1899.
The numbers on the pendant are the acquisition number given to the item by museum personnel.

A commemorative medallion, minted in Europe, showing General Botha's portrait.

The Battle of Spioenkop, 24 January 1900

For General Redvers Buller, there was no talk of giving up, his defeat at Colenso notwithstanding. Ladysmith had to be relieved: he set out on a second attempt in January 1900 with a 4 000-strong force.

Buller ordered an attack on Spioenkop, a large hill in the centre of the Boer line, near Ladysmith, on the night of 23 January. Major General Edward Woodgate, at the head of 2 000 men, was given the task. If Woodgate could take Spioenkop, his men could then cover Buller's push to Ladysmith with artillery and small-arms fire.

Woodgate's men surprised a small group of sleeping Boers, and, with cries of 'Avenge Majuba!', drove them off with little effort.

A pocket watch engraved with the ZAR coat of arms. It belonged to 22-year-old Johannes Petrus Bothma of the Carolina commando, who perished on Spioenkop. The watch was found during excavations in 1978.

Woodgate ordered his men to dig in as close to the top of the hill as possible, and to conceal themselves well despite the rain and mist: he wanted to surprise the Boers. To move as silently as possible, his men left most of their equipment at the foot of the hill. This, however, made it impossible for them to dig in too deeply in the rocky terrain; instead they dug a shallow trench and erected a low wall.

When the mist cleared, they realised their positions were 80 to 200 paces below the ridge on the northern slope. This would restrict their range of fire.

Knowing how important the hill was to the British plan of attack, General Louis Botha had to act quickly. He ordered a 400-man force, headed by Commandant Hendrik Prinsloo of the Carolina commando and Commandant 'Rooi' Daniël Opperman of the Pretoria commando, to storm Spioenkop in thick mist. They fought hand to hand with British defenders on the northeastern slope, while Boer positions directed their artillery and Mauser fire at the British positions on Spioenkop.

White handkerchiefs were soon waved. The Boers ceased fire, only to come under British fire again shortly afterwards. By the afternoon, with Woodgate badly wounded and his exhausted men running out of water, the British were in trouble. The Boers, relentless, continued their artillery bombardment and heavy crossfire.

The call came to evacuate. The Boers reoccupied Spioenkop the following morning. The shrapnel wound above Woodgate's eye would claim his life two months later.

The boots of 25-year-old Lambertus Lochner (Lammie) de Villiers of the Pretoria commando, who died in the Battle of Spioenkop.

In his book *London to Ladysmith via Pretoria*, Winston Churchill described the scene at Spioenkop as follows: 'Streams of wounded met us and obstructed the path. Men were staggering along alone, or supported by comrades, or crawling on hands and knees, or carried by stretchers. Corpses lay here and there. Many of the wounds were of a horrible nature. The splinters and fragments of the shells had torn and mutilated in the most ghastly manner.' He continued: 'The Lancashire Fusiliers, the Imperial Light Infantry – whose baptism of fire it was – Thorneycroft's, and the Middlesex Regiment sustained the greater part of the loss. We will have another try, and, if it pleases God, do better next time.'

Britain's international standing did not survive the Spioenkop defeat unscathed. Botha, on the other hand, had proved himself as a military strategist. But without either side realising it, Spioenkop signalled a turning point in the war; the republicans would soon be unable to match Britain's military might.

A sword taken from a British soldier during the Battle of Spioenkop.

General Louis Botha (circled) on Spioenkop after the battle.

ABOVE A Boer commando shortly after the Battle of Spioenkop.

BELOW About 240 British soldiers perished on Spioenkop. At the time, Winston Churchill, then a war correspondent, described Spioenkop as 'another Majuba' for Britain.

The Battle of Paardeberg, 18 February 1900

The Boers' siege strategy, which may have been successful in the war's early stages, had unintended consequences: it gave Britain time to ship many thousands of additional troops to South Africa, troops who would descend upon, and relieve, Ladysmith, Kimberley and Mafeking.

When Lord Roberts replaced General Redvers Buller as British commander in chief, he restrategised, planning attacks on the republics' capital cities from the western front.

Once Lieutenant General John French had relieved Kimberley on 15 February 1900, General Piet Cronjé left his Magersfontein positions for new ones, moving eastward along the Modder River. Two days later, a British force under Lord Kitchener cornered Cronjé near Paardeberg, on the north bank of the river. (Kitchener had taken Roberts's place, as the latter was indisposed.)

Cronjé refused to abandon his convoy of 400 ox-wagons, or the nearly 50 women and children in his care. So, he dug in along the river with his 4 000-odd men.

With the 15 000 troops and numerous pieces of artillery that he had at his disposal, Kitchener stormed Cronjé's positions from three sides under cover of heavy bombardment. The British were repelled time and again, suffering heavy losses: 303 perished, 906 were wounded and 61 were captured. Boer losses numbered about 70 dead and wounded.

Lord Roberts, now recovered, continued the siege of Cronjé's positions, sustaining a heavy artillery bombardment for over a week. General Christiaan de Wet reached the battlefield on 18 February and tried in vain to relieve Cronjé. In the face of enormous danger, Danie Theron of the Reconnaissance Corps managed to get a message from De Wet through to Cronjé.

An American pine *riempie* chair (made from leather thongs) that belonged to General Piet Cronjé, plundered by a British officer. Years later, the officer's sister-in-law, CV Chapman, sent the chair to the War Museum from England.

An inkpot from Piet Cronjé's writing desk, taken as a souvenir by a British soldier after the Battle of Paardeberg. ✒

Disarray at Paardeberg following the capitulation. Roberts's forces destroyed the encampment by shooting it to pieces, fearing an outbreak of dysentery; over 4 000 people had lived in unsanitary conditions there.

De Wet failed to talk Cronjé into breaking out of the siege without his wagons and the women and children, however.

De Wet's attacks on British positions caused enough confusion for a handful of the besieged to make their escape, including the well-known seer Siener van Rensburg. The British bombardment of Cronjé's laager continued. The republican fighters dug shelters into the banks of the Modder River, where the lack of sanitation, rotting animal carcasses and Orange Free State heat worsened conditions by the day.

Observation balloons allowed British artillery to target Cronjé's positions with extreme accuracy. The situation, inevitably, became hopeless. De Wet could only watch as Cronjé handed himself and his 4 000 men – about 10 per cent of the total republican fighting force – over to Roberts

on 27 February, the anniversary of the British defeat at Majuba, in 1881, during the First War of Independence.

How the tables had turned.

In the book *The Boer War*, a British soldier describes Cronjé's capitulation as follows: 'Cronje rode in on a grey bony horse, seeming in his old green overcoat, frieze trousers, rough veldschoen boots and slouch-hat even bulkier by contrast with the neat little field-marshal. At the moment Cronje dismounted and Roberts stepped forward, a camera clicked ... Roberts stepped forward to shake hands. He said: "I am glad to see you. You have made a gallant defence, sir."'

Boer morale plummeted; not only had many burghers become prisoners of war, but the way had also been cleared for an assault on Bloemfontein.

ABOVE General Piet Cronjé.

LEFT This unique Vierkleur, called the 'Immanuel' flag, was made by Boer women and given to Cronjé at the start of the war. The flag was unfurled at the Battle of Magersfontein and was also hoisted in Cronjé's laager at Paardeberg.

The Republican Capitals Under Siege

Bloemfontein

In March 1900, about five months after the first shot had been fired in the Anglo-Boer War, Boer defences in the Orange Free State began to crumble. Kimberley had been relieved, and General Piet Cronjé had surrendered at Paardeberg. The Boer forces' western front had collapsed.

The Boer contingent in the southern Orange Free State feared being cornered too, and fell back to the eastern part of the republic. This led to the collapse of the southern front.

The Orange Free State administration made preparations in early March to move the government – including its archives, materiel and treasury – out of Bloemfontein. A Commission for Public Safety was formed of Bloemfontein residents to maintain law and order in the government's absence. On 12 March 1900, the Free State government left Bloemfontein for Kroonstad, and this northern Free State town was proclaimed the republic's new capital.

Meanwhile, British units had started putting railway and telegraph lines out of commission. Lord Roberts levelled a 'formal demand for surrender' at the town; the republicans declined to respond.

Residents and merchants steeled themselves for a siege. German traders barricaded their shop windows, and Union Jacks appeared as if from nowhere. British artillery fired a few salvos at the town.

Journalists from several newspapers streamed in, pre-empting the British army; it is not for nothing that the Anglo-Boer War was seen as the world's first 'media war'. Daredevil British journalists Percival Landon from *The Times*, HA Gwynne from Reuters and 'Banjo' Patterson from *The Sydney Morning Herald* talked the Commission for Public Safety into riding out to meet Lord Roberts and handing over the town officially. Roberts would later say that it was the press, essentially, that conquered Bloemfontein.

Resident Sophie Leviseur recounted that a colourful British army vanguard, flags and ensigns fluttering, marched down Church Street on 13 March at 1 pm – complete with pipers, lords,

A range of patriotic waltzes, marches, solos and other light music was composed in the British Empire during the war, and published in the form of sheet music. Fabian Scott was known for his piano compositions called 'Bloemfontein March', 'A Night Attack' and 'Pretoria March'.

officers atop prancing horses, foreign military attachés and Roberts's Indian valets.

The occupying force was impressive: 33 954 soldiers, 11 450 horses, mules, and carriages – including the Royal Field Artillery's guns and naval guns from HMS *Doris* and HMS *Monarch* – raised a dust trail several miles long.

Residents recall how the foot soldiers looked more like tramps than conquerors in their tattered uniforms. Many showed early signs of dysentery from drinking contaminated water from the Modder River following the Battle of Paardeberg.

The procession came to halt before the bust of Jan Brand, fourth state president of the republic. Roberts read the inscription on Brand's monument, and saluted it. The British high command then took up residence in the Presidency, while the troops made camp on the farm Tempe, on the outskirts of the town.

During a short ceremony, the Union Jack was hoisted at the Presidency. Made of silk, the flag was presented by Lady Nora Roberts.

ABOVE Lord Roberts's troops enter Bloemfontein. After the Orange Free State was annexed, it was renamed the Orange River Colony.

BELOW British troops on Hoffman Square in Bloemfontein in May 1900 after the annexation of the Orange Free State. *Western Cape Archives*

Roberts's march on Pretoria would have to wait: the poor condition of his army, and the wave of dysentery that swept through it, prolonged his Orange Free State sojourn. With rail links damaged, food and materiel were soon in short supply.

On his departure from South Africa, Lord Roberts took several souvenirs
with him, including the Presidency's silver cutlery set and porcelain crockery
(above), as well as the Steyns' personal silver cutlery (fork and soup ladle
above). After his death, his widow, Lady Nora Roberts, returned the remaining
pieces to South Africa. These remnants ended up at Groote Schuur in Cape
Town, the prime minister's official residence. Tibbie Steyn, President MT Steyn's
widow, is reputed to have recognised the items at a state banquet at Groote
Schuur in 1919 – and to have asked for their return. They were sent by train
to Bloemfontein, but all the knives were lost in transit.

Pretoria

On 7 May 1900, the Eerste Volksraad of the South African Republic met for the last time. Wreaths were laid on the seats of Volksraad members such as Michiel Kock, who had perished in battle; the Vierkleur was draped over the seat of the captured Piet Cronjé. Preparations had already been made to evacuate the government.

Lord Roberts and his triumphant army marched into Johannesburg on 31 May 1900 after the city surrendered to the British forces. After resting there for a few days, they resumed the march on Pretoria.

President Kruger and a handful of administrators and Executive Council members had boarded a train for Machadodorp, the newly proclaimed seat of government, a day earlier. Shortly before the occupation of Pretoria, Attorney General Jan Smuts emptied the state coffers' last reserves, loading about half a million pounds in currency and gold bars onto one of the last trains to leave. British shells had already started pounding the suburb of Sunnyside and the area around Pretoria station. (This is the origin of the legend of the hidden Kruger millions, which have led to several unsuccessful searches.)

Commandant General Louis Botha's commandos retreated eastwards with a few pieces of artillery. One of Botha's final tasks before leaving the town himself was to appoint a committee of

British troops enter the outskirts of Pretoria on horseback. *Western Cape Archives*

A boutonnière like this one was sent to each member of the Worcestershire Yeomanry. The note reads: 'From Lady Dudley, with best wishes for the Worcestershire Yeomanry, to wear on entering Pretoria.'

residents to maintain law and order: by then, some residents had already started looting the state's military stores, and anarchy loomed. The women of Pretoria honoured Botha one last time by presenting him with a silk scarf embroidered with the words 'Strijdt met Gods Hulp'.

The *Morning Post*'s Winston Churchill was among the British media anticipating a battle with the guns of the four forts around Pretoria. Roberts readied his heavy-calibre guns, firing a few shots towards Fort Schanskop. His suspicions were confirmed, and the journalists bitterly disappointed, when he met no resistance: the forts' Long Toms had long since been deployed in the field, leaving them toothless.

Roberts and about 20 000 men rode into Pretoria from the south on 5 June 1900. Receiving his contingent's salute on Church Square at 2 pm consummated his ambitions: he had occupied the capitals of the Boer republics. Cheered on by thousands of soldiers and a few residents, Lady Roberts's embroidered Union Jack was unfurled before the Raadsaal.

The British government and high command in South Africa were certain that the war was over. Little did they know what lay ahead.

The Cape and Natal Rebels

When war broke out, many Afrikaners in the Cape and Natal, both British colonies, were torn between their loyalty to the Crown and their elected governments, and their cultural and familial ties to fellow Afrikaners in the Boer republics.

When the Boer republics invaded the two colonies, about 10 000 Afrikaner rebels took up arms against the British government. By early 1900, when the Boer commandos had been driven back to the republics, these rebels were permitted to return to the colonies – provided they laid down their weapons.

Most took advantage of the amnesty, but some continued to fight in the republican forces even if they faced a court martial and possible execution if caught.

Martial law (or 'Martjie Louw', as Afrikaners termed it) was declared early – on 16 October 1899 – in the parts of the Cape Colony that bordered the Orange Free State. Its reach spread as the commandos moved deeper into the colony. Natal followed the same pattern, declaring martial law initially in border regions and later across the whole colony.

By early February 1901, martial law had been declared in every district of the Cape Colony. The British military forced farmers to hand over any items that could aid the republican war effort, including horses and mules.

Saddles, carriages, carts and even pliers, nails and horseshoes had to be relinquished. In some districts, farmers were even forbidden to sow crops; they were allowed to keep food stores for only 14 days – and sometimes just one week – in their homes.

Rebels whom the British army captured were imprisoned or fined, although some were banished. A total of 44 rebels captured in the Cape Colony were tried and executed.

To deter prospective rebels, the British military command ordered sentencing to take place publicly, in areas where the rebels had carried out their attacks.

This pocket watch belonged to Johannes Petrus Coetzee. At just 16, Coetzee was the youngest rebel to be sentenced to death; he was executed by British military authorities on 13 July 1901 at Cradock. The watch was discovered in his grave during his reburial.

A hat belonging to WM Meyer, a Cape rebel from Pearson, taken as a prisoner of war at Vryburg in 1900. Note the drawings of the republican flags, and the inscriptions showing the dates on which he was tried and the jails in which he was detained.

The barrel of the Long Tom gun that was damaged during the Siege of Ladysmith. Here it is being repaired in the workshop of the Nederlandsch-Zuid-Afrikaansche Spoorwegmaatschappij (a Dutch railway company) in Pretoria. The repairs included shortening the barrel.

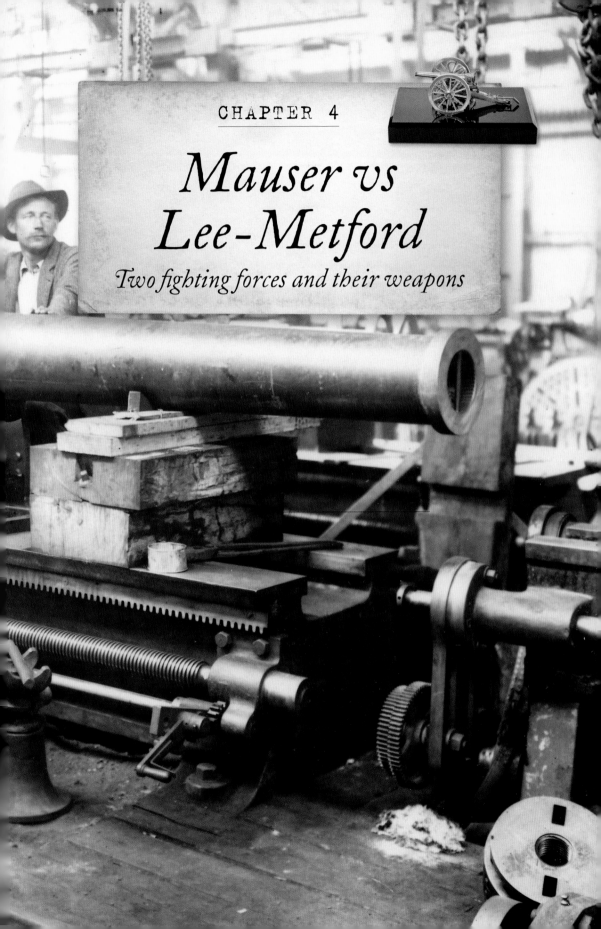

CHAPTER 4

Mauser vs Lee-Metford

Two fighting forces and their weapons

Tommy Atkins — the British soldier

The Britain of 1899 may have boasted a thriving middle class, but most Britons were working class. Inadequate schooling saw many working-class Britons enter the labour market at a young age; their employment in the mining, industrial and agricultural sectors was not always well paid.

The British Army and Royal Navy offered many of these a fixed income and a better life. Adventure in the unknown beckoned! These everyman figures came to be known colloquially as Tommy Atkins (the typical British soldier) and Jack Tar (the typical British sailor).

When the Anglo-Boer War broke out, Tommy Atkins marched, to the tune of 'Rule, Britannia' and other patriotic songs, through the streets of Britain's towns and cities straight to an unknown land on the southern tip of Africa.

The class divide between officers and soldiers in the British Army was cavernous. Most British officers hailed from the middle class and gentry,

British troops and artillery arrive in South Africa shortly after war was declared.
Western Cape Archives

and they dominated the command of the three branches of the army (infantry, cavalry and artillery). Tommy Atkins's career prospects were severely limited.

The average Boer fighter was part of a people's army that had a less formal hierarchical structure that was also not followed as strictly; in contrast, the British foot soldier was expected, in the words of one historian, 'to obey rigid instructions to the last syllable, to keep splendid order, and to let his superiors do the thinking for him'.

During the war's second phase, infantryman Tommy Atkins remade himself as a mounted infantryman. He had never ridden a horse before; the learning curve was steep. A British officer once drily referred to the mounted infantry as 'cavalry gone bad'.

With his poor training and antiquated military techniques, Tommy Atkins — the lowly foot soldier — was ill-suited to war in southern Africa. He also paid the highest price during the first phase of the combat — during the occupation of Bloemfontein, for example — when dysentery swept through the ranks.

An item that belonged to Private A Howard of the 1st Battalion, Royal Dublin Fusiliers. This Irish regiment took part in the battles at Talana, Colenso, Venterspruit, Vaalkrans, Hart's Hill, Pieters Hill and Graskop.

A British officer during the war.

A British soldier of the mounted infantry, taken during the guerrilla phase of the war. The slouch hat that replaced the pith helmet in 1901 sometimes saw British soldiers on patrol being mistaken for Boer commandos, and sometimes even coming under friendly fire.

Queen Victoria sent tins like this one, also containing six small chocolate bars, to all her soldiers in South Africa. A total of 123 000 tins were distributed on 1 January 1900. The chocolates were manufactured by the confectionery firms Cadbury, Fry and Rowntree. Cadbury did not want to make any profit from the chocolate and therefore donated their contribution. Mohandas Karamchand Gandhi, who founded the Natal Indian Ambulance Corps and later went on to lead the struggle for Indian independence, objected to the fact that none of the Indian volunteers, who served as stretcher-bearers, received the tins. 🔫

Boer Fighters and the Commandos

The Orange Free State and Transvaal based their forces on the commando system, which dated back to the period of Dutch East India Company rule in the Cape. In the absence of a permanent military force, burghers were permitted to organise to protect themselves and their property.

The commando system was especially valuable during the numerous conflicts between Cape border farmers and Xhosa groups. The system chiefly comprised a mounted citizen force. The Voortrekkers used this system during the Great Trek of 1838, and applied it in the territories that became the republics. Its rank structure was refined over the years: the Company period's 'field corporal' became 'field cornet', for example.

The Orange Free State formalised the commando system in 1866 by passing a commando law. The Transvaal had similar legislation. According to the law, every able-bodied male between the ages of 16 and 60 who could handle a rifle was a member of the citizen force and could thus be conscripted into it.

The republics were divided into districts. Each district had its own commando; commando sizes varied from 300 to 3 000 men. Districts were further divided into wards. An elected commandant headed each commando, assisted by elected field cornets. Each field cornet was responsible for his own ward; assistant field cornets were appointed in larger wards.

Transvaal commandos were headed by an elected commandant general. In the Orange Free State, an elected chief commandant headed the commandos during wartime. Both republics used war councils to make military decisions.

An important advantage of the commandos was that they were highly mobile and very quick to muster. Each member used his own weapon, horse and saddle, and was legally required to participate in frequent target-shooting exercises. The first eight days' rations were the commando member's responsibility. Thereafter, the onus to provide rations fell on the state.

The commando system's loose discipline was a source of great frustration for Boer generals, as many Boers would return temporarily to their farms during military operations.

During the war's guerrilla phase, all able-bodied men who could bear arms – from the unproven seven-year-old youngster to the old-timer of 70 – were welcomed on commando. Commando law stated that black people could be called up as helpers to perform support roles. These so-called *agterryers* (grooms) were at times also armed and a few even took part in battle.

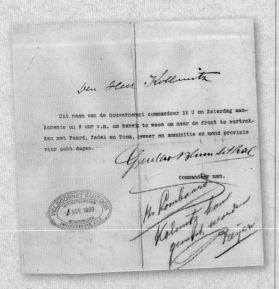

Call-up papers for citizen Hugo Kollmitz to report with horse, saddle and bridle, rifle and ammunition, and rations for eight days to go on commando.

SOUTH AFRICAN REPUBLIC COMMANDOS

Bethal, Bloemhof, Boksburg, Carolina, Ermelo, Germiston, Heidelberg, Johannesburg, Krugersdorp, Lichtenburg, Lydenburg, Marico, Middelburg, Piet Retief, Potchefstroom, Pretoria, Rustenburg, Standerton, Swaziland, Utrecht, Vryheid, Wakkerstroom, Waterberg, Wolmaransstad and Soutpansberg.

ORANGE FREE STATE COMMANDOS

Bethlehem, Bethulie, Bloemfontein, Boshof, Fauresmith, Ficksburg, Harrismith, Heilbron, Hoopstad, Jacobsdal, Kroonstad, Ladybrand, Philippolis, Rouxville, Senekal, Thaba Nchu, Smithfield, Vrede, Wepener and Winburg.

Citizen HJR van Niekerk's waistcoat, modified to hold bullets.

The British Army in South Africa

The Anglo-Boer War was not only the last war that Great Britain fought under Queen Victoria's rule; it was also Britain's last imperial war.

The Boer republics' ultimatum caught the Salisbury government somewhat unawares. Britain was still busy supplementing the garrison in South Africa, because at that time the republics had the numerical advantage. During the war's first phase, then, the British army was forced into a defensive strategy.

The republics' advantage would be short-lived, however. As British numbers grew, offensive tactics came into play.

Sir Redvers Buller was Britain's first appointment to the South African high command. His strategy involved invading the republics from Natal. After Black Week (10–17 December 1899, when Britain suffered three devastating defeats at Stormberg, Magersfontein and Colenso), Lord Roberts replaced Buller. Roberts chose to attack the Boer republics from the Cape Colony.

The British army in South Africa had three branches:

- The infantry (foot soldiers and, later, the mounted infantry), the largest part of the army. The infantry mostly comprised Rifles, Fusiliers, Highlanders, Borderers and Guards regiments;
- The cavalry, including mounted regiments such as Lancers, Hussars and Dragoons; and
- The artillery corps, consisting of the Royal Field Artillery (RFA), the Royal Horse Artillery (RHA, a mobile unit with lighter ordnance) and the Royal Garrison Artillery, which included heavy ordnance such as that found at fortresses and shore batteries.

Supporting the army in the field were the Royal Army Medical Corps, the Army Service Corps (which provided for the army's transport requirements), the Army Ordnance Department (which supplied the army's military provisions) and the Royal Engineers (which repaired damaged infrastructure such as bridges and tunnels, and erected military structures such as blockhouses).

Smaller supplemental units in the army included the Royal Army Chaplains Department, the Royal Army Veterinary Corps, the Army Pay Department, the Military Police and the Army Nursing Services.

Black Week saw volunteer units, such as the Imperial Yeomanry and the London Imperial Volunteers, come into being in Britain.

Over and above this, the British war effort was supplemented by contributions from British colonies and territories, including Australia, Canada, New Zealand and Bechuanaland (now Botswana), as well as from the Cape Colony and Natal. Smaller units of white soldiers were sent from Burma (now Myanmar), Ceylon (now Sri Lanka) and India.

A number of volunteer units were raised in the Cape Colony and Natal, including Brabant's Horse, Bethune's Mounted Infantry, the Umvoti Mounted Rifles and the Natal Field Artillery. In addition, police forces from the two colonies made a contribution, as did support units such as the Railway Pioneer Corps, which was largely responsible for repairing damaged rail links. The Town Guard was founded to protect towns from Boer commando attacks.

In the war's final phase, British military authorities also came to depend on Boers who had switched sides in the conflict. These took the

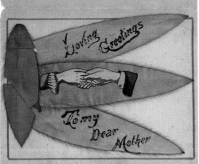

One Private Smith sent this postcard to his family in Britain. On the one side are dried protea leaves and on the other is an illustration of the Battle of Stormberg. This illustration is part of a series of illustrations of different battles, such as those at Elandslaagte, Spioenkop, Magersfontein and Colenso, that were drawn in the Netherlands.

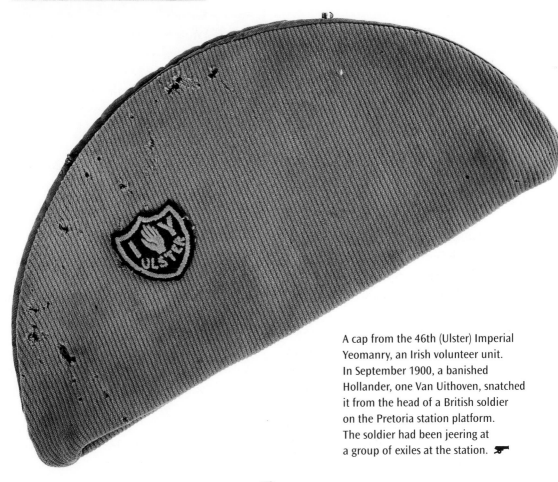

A cap from the 46th (Ulster) Imperial Yeomanry, an Irish volunteer unit. In September 1900, a banished Hollander, one Van Uithoven, snatched it from the head of a British soldier on the Pretoria station platform. The soldier had been jeering at a group of exiles at the station.

form of the Orange River Colony Volunteers in the Orange Free State, and the National Scouts in the Transvaal. These Boers' knowledge of the terrain was hugely valuable to the British.

Black South Africans also played an important role in the British war effort, serving in paid labour forces. The British military command gradually armed them, deploying them in combat and also as spies, runners, drivers and guards.

The experience of the Anglo-Boer War led to many British army reforms. Engagement at the southern tip of Africa opened the generals' eyes to new tactics and strategies that would be put to use during the First World War.

A pocket watch that belonged to a British soldier. The soldier was badly wounded in battle by one burgher Marais, who was also wounded. Marais took the watch from him. Note the bullet attached to the chain, which hit Marais in the femur. The inscription 'P.L.S.D.C.O. Yeomanry' is engraved on the back of the watch.

The British Navy

The Royal Navy's South Atlantic squadron had several warships, such as cruisers and gunboats, at its disposal. When war broke out, however, seven first-class cruisers, including HMS *Terrible* and HMS *Powerful*, were sent as reinforcements.

Vice Admiral Sir Robert Harris, commanding the Cape of Good Hope Station, was tasked with preventing any materiel originating in Europe from reaching the republics via the port of Lourenço Marques. His decision to search European merchant ships at sea drew heavy criticism: in one case, a German ship, the *Herzog*, was intercepted by a British warship and escorted to a harbour, where it was searched.

Ironically, the British navy's most significant contribution to the conflict was on land. British artillery was no match, initially, for the Boers' Long Toms, and so deploying their ships' heavy ordnance became a necessity.

At short notice, Captain PM Scott of HMS *Terrible* built chassis for HMS *Powerful* and HMS *Terrible*'s naval guns (and, later, for those of HMS *Monarch* and HMS *Doris*). These naval guns, manned by the Naval Brigade, played an important role in the Siege of Ladysmith and the battles at Graspan and Magersfontein.

HMS *Penelope*, an ageing armoured corvette, also housed Boer prisoners of war temporarily. During their invasion of the Cape Colony, Boer commandos exchanged fire with British warships on the Cape west coast on three occasions.

Crew of HMS *Niobe*, one of the Royal Navy's first-class cruisers. The vessel was part of the reinforcements that Britain sent to the Cape when war broke out. HMS *Niobe* also escorted the ship that transported prisoner of war Piet Cronjé to St Helena. 🔫

Forts in the South African Republic and Orange Free State

Pretoria and Johannesburg

In 1896, the Jameson Raid brought home to the Volksraad, the parliament of the South African Republic, just how vulnerable the republic was to attack, both from without and from within. The government was concerned about the number of Uitlanders in the Transvaal, fearing Pretoria's vulnerability in particular.

Leon Grunberg, a French artillery specialist, proposed a plan to fortify the town by building eight forts, each with a rotating gun turret. The high cost of the exercise saw only four forts being built, however.

Three of the four forts around Pretoria – Forts Klapperkop, Schanskop and Wonderboompoort – were German designs. The fourth, Fort Daspoort, was a French design. This fort was only completed in 1898, shortly before the outbreak of war. The primary weaponry in all four forts was the 155-mm siege gun, manufactured by the French firm Schneider, widely known as the 'Long Tom'.

At the time of construction, the structures met the latest requirements for fortifications and were built using the best-quality materials available, such as Krupp steel from Germany. However, between design and completion, advances were made in the development of explosives. The new generation of explosives, such as lyddite and meinite, could potentially damage the forts. All four were equipped with running water and up-to-date services, such as electricity and a telephone system.

Shortly before the war, a fifth fort was erected in Johannesburg, primarily to help suppress any unrest that could develop within the town.

The British brought their own heavy artillery to bombard the forts when they captured Pretoria. With the Long Toms deployed in the field, however, the forts lay unprotected. The Royal Engineers took them over, and they assumed a new role as part of the British defence system around Pretoria.

British troops at the entrance to Johannesburg Fort. Note the South African Republic coat of arms above the entrance. Today, the site is the home of the Constitutional Court of South Africa.

Bloemfontein

Henry Warden, Bloemfontein's founder, built Fort Bloemfontein, a humble ironstone and earth-embankment structure, in 1848. Initially known as Queen's Fort, it was rechristened Fort Bloemfontein when the Republic of the Orange Free State came into being in 1854.

The Orange Free State Artillery Corps was headquartered at the fort. Reinforcements and improvements over the years notwithstanding, the Orange Free State Volksraad acknowledged that the fort would not survive an attack using modern ordnance. The decision was made to erect a better, more modern fortification on Signal Hill in Bloemfontein, but the project stalled.

When the city fell to the British, the Coldstream Guards occupied Fort Bloemfontein; the Union Jack flew over it once again, after 46 years. Later in the war, the fort was the headquarters of the South African Constabulary, the Orange Free State division of the British police force.

This heliograph was used on commando by the Bittereinder Adriaan van der Heever. The artillerymen stationed in the four forts around Pretoria communicated using heliographs, telephones and telegraphic apparatus.

This heliographer was photographed at Kraaipan, where the first battle of the Anglo-Boer War took place.

Boer Communication in the Field

by Dané Swanepoel

During the Anglo-Boer War, communication was wireless; Morse code was used, with the help of signal flags and flickering (or reflecting) light. So, signalmen were trained in the use of flags, heliographs, oil lamps and carbide lamps.

The Orange Free State Artillery Corps had been using signalling equipment since 1885. In August 1899, with war clouds gathering, President MT Steyn decided to establish heliograph stations between the Orange Free State and the Transvaal. Free State artillerymen used red and white flags, but, given the background of mountains and hilltops against which they signalled, this communication medium had limited success.

When war broke out, the Orange Free State and Transvaal signalmen moved with the commandos; each commando had more than one heliograph. A heliograph team usually consisted of three heliographers, who signalled, interpreted and received messages, respectively.

The field heliograph worked well during the day, when signalmen could use sunlight to transmit messages. At night, they could send signals with the help of a lantern, but these signals did not travel far.

The shortage of signalmen meant that young boys were often called upon to serve. In many cases, the heliograph would be manned by a single person, who had to receive, interpret and transcribe the signals by himself.

When signalmen realised that their messages were being intercepted, they frequently used new codes, and scrambled them as well, to prevent the British from decrypting their communications.

British forces plundered this field telephone, with its custom-made leather case, at Lindley. It was used by General Christiaan de Wet's commando.

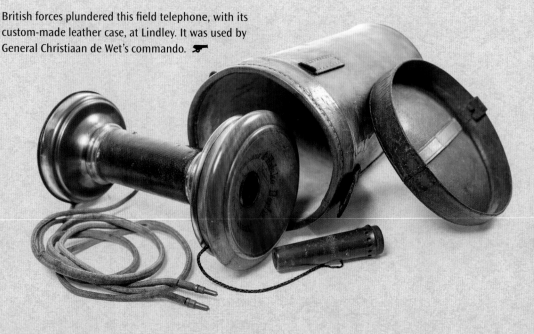

A War in Images

by Etna Labuschagne

The vast photographic record of the Anglo-Boer War has seen it being dubbed the world's first major media war. A number of amateur and professional photographers on both sides of the conflict helped to record this piece of history in images.

During the war, professional photographers were sent to the battlefields to photograph the combatants. Soldiers were also instructed by photographers to pose for photos. These treasured mementoes were then sent to family members and friends, who anxiously waited for news from the battlefronts.

British magazines such as *Black & White Budget* sent photographers to South Africa specifically to take photos at the front. Their photos were put up on the walls of music halls in London and in other places, to arouse feelings of patriotism.

The Kodak box camera, which used rolled film, had entered the market in 1888, making photography accessible to the general public for the first time. Thanks to this development, soldiers could take cameras to the front and document military activities in the field. For instance, at the Battle of Modder River, Sir Henry Colvile documented a number of scenes using his box camera.

A number of amateur photographers therefore found themselves among the British troops. Due to the long exposure times these early cameras required, most of the shots were posed. Later, shorter exposure times allowed action shots to be taken.

The photographic collection of the War Museum of the Boer Republics consists of about 7 500 images. This includes original material such as daguerreotypes and so-called lantern slides. Other images are copies of originals owned by private individuals or copies from newspapers and other publications.

The collection also contains numerous stereograph images, including those taken by Reinhold Thiele of the *Daily Graphic*. Stereograph photos were printed in pairs and were viewed with a special instrument, the stereoscope (see object on title page). The stereoscope had two lenses that caused the two images to merge when you looked through the instrument, creating a three-dimensional image. During this era, looking at stereograph photos was a popular form of entertainment at parties.

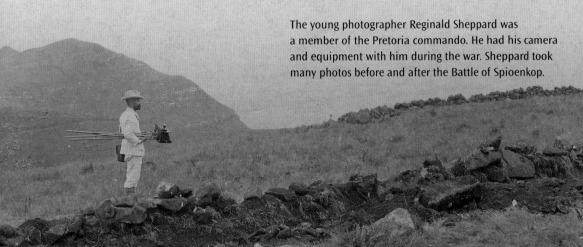

The young photographer Reginald Sheppard was a member of the Pretoria commando. He had his camera and equipment with him during the war. Sheppard took many photos before and after the Battle of Spioenkop.

Boer Weapons: the Mauser

by Ron Bester

The two Boer republics each had a small police and artillery force, but no permanent army, relying instead on citizen forces in times of war. Both republics had commando laws that regulated the organisation of these forces and specified that all able-bodied citizens aged 16 to 60 had to be prepared for commando service.

It was every eligible citizen's duty to acquire a rifle and ammunition. Authorities assisted less-resourced citizens in this by purchasing rifles wholesale and selling them at reasonable prices.

The Transvaal government officially imported a range of rifles, including the Martini-Henry, Guedes, Krag-Jörgenson and Mauser. The Orange Free State government's preference was for Westley Richards breech-loading rifles, Martini-Henrys and Mausers.

Weapon acquisitions gained pace after the failed Jameson Raid. From 1896 to the onset of hostilities in October 1899, the South African Republic largely obtained Martini-Henrys and Mausers for their citizen forces and the Free State Mausers.

The Boer Mauser was a unique variation of the Spanish Model 1893 Mauser. It used the 7×57-mm round. As the name suggests, the weapon was developed by German rifle specialist Paul Mauser. The South African Republic ordered 20 000 long Mausers from Germany in 1896, along with 5 000 similar carbines. In 1897, an order was placed for another 10 000 long Mausers and 2 000 carbines.

Like the British Lee-Metford/Enfield, the Boer Mauser was a bolt-action rifle with a five-round magazine. The Mauser magazine took fewer rounds than the ten-shot Lee magazine, but could handle a higher rate of fire because a new magazine could be loaded in a single action with the help of a clip.

The Mauser assisted Boer fighters to gain a reputation for being excellent marksmen. Testimonies abound of practically impossible shots that Boers took accurately with their Mausers. Many Boers beautified their Mausers with elaborate engravings on their rifle stocks.

Without a doubt, the Mauser was the superior weapon: after the war, the British Army undertook changes to the Lees that only the Mauser could have inspired. They went even further to design the Pattern 14 Mauser, which itself inspired the American Model 17. About 75 per cent of American troops in the First World War were equipped with this rifle.

A father and his sons with their Mausers shortly after the outbreak of the war.

Two Boer Mausers, one with calligraphy and the other with carving on the stock. Subjects carved on Boer rifle stocks included names, birthplaces, dates of birth, the battles in which they had participated and the republican flags.

Mauser rounds were packed in clips of five. The Boer Mauser action was designed in such a way that the clip fitted into a small slot on the back of the weapon. To load the magazine with five rounds, the clip was placed in this slot. The shooter then used a single downward movement of his thumb to push all five rounds into the magazine. The empty clip was then ejected when the bolt was closed. In this way, the Mauser could sustain a much higher rate of fire than the Lee-Metford/Enfield.

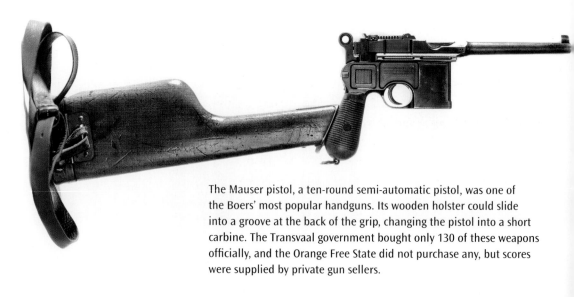

The Mauser pistol, a ten-round semi-automatic pistol, was one of the Boers' most popular handguns. Its wooden holster could slide into a groove at the back of the grip, changing the pistol into a short carbine. The Transvaal government bought only 130 of these weapons officially, and the Orange Free State did not purchase any, but scores were supplied by private gun sellers.

British Weapons:
.303 Lee-Metford/Enfield

by Ron Bester

In 1888, Great Britain started using the Lee-Metford rifle, which fired a smaller-calibre, .303 inch (7.7-mm) round. The rifle was named for the inventor of the action (James Paris Lee) and the designer of the barrel type (William Metford). Seven shallow grooves characterise the Metford barrel, which was well suited to the earliest, gunpowder-loaded .303 rounds.

Propellants developed as rifles did. Over time, the .303 rounds came to be filled with the modern, smokeless gunpowder known as cordite. Cordite-loaded rounds combusted at a higher temperature than ordinary gunpowder ones, however. The shallow-grooved Metford barrels quickly became shot out when cordite-loaded rounds were used.

The Enfield barrel later replaced the Metford barrel. Its five deeper, angled grooves were better suited to cordite-loaded rounds. This led to the development of the Lee-Enfield in 1895.

Whereas the name 'Enfield' came from the British arsenal at Enfield Lock, north London, the Enfield barrel was also developed by Metford. The Lee-Metfords and Lee-Enfields, collectively called 'Lees', came in two lengths: a longer rifle for foot soldiers, measuring 49½ inches, and a shorter carbine for mounted forces and artillery, measuring 39^{15}/₁₆ inches.

The first Lee-Metford – the Mark I – was created in 1888. The long version underwent several minor changes, but only more significant changes constituted a change in the mark. The small improvements were signalled by a star at the end of the mark name – for example, Mark I*. The larger improvements resulted in a new mark – for example, Mark II.

At the beginning of the war, most British soldiers carried Mark I*, Mark II and, to a lesser extent, Mark II* Lee-Metfords. The more modern Lee-Enfields reached South Africa over time; by the end of the war, the Lee-Enfield Mark I and Mark I* were in common use.

The basic Lee – a bolt-action magazine rifle – was extremely robust, used by the British Empire not only during the Anglo-Boer War but also in the two World Wars. Aside from the Lee-Metford Mark I, which had an eight-round magazine, all long Lees had a ten-round magazine.

Lee carbines had six-round magazines. In contrast to the Mauser, the Lee's empty magazines had to be reloaded one round at a time.

The sights of the Lees left a lot to be desired, and they were difficult to aim: the tops of the barrels were not clad with wood, which not only burnt the soldiers' hands in combat but also created a heat haze that hampered their ability to take aim.

A long Lee-Metford Mark II, used most commonly by British troops at the beginning of the war.

The Pattern 1888 was the standard bayonet for all long Lee-Metfords/Enfields used in the war. There were three variations; this is the Mark I, second model. Bayonets played a negligible role in the war.

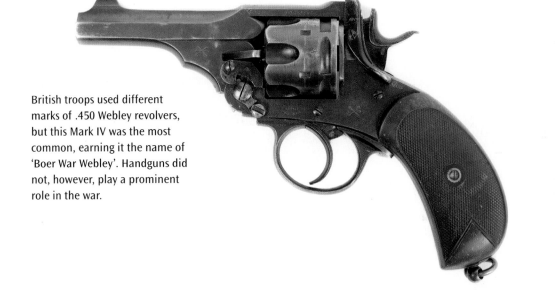

British troops used different marks of .450 Webley revolvers, but this Mark IV was the most common, earning it the name of 'Boer War Webley'. Handguns did not, however, play a prominent role in the war.

On the left is a cordite Mark II, the standard .303 round that British troops used in South Africa. The stamps on the round show the manufacturer code and the C II mark (Cordite Mark II). Despite both sides of the conflict having forbidden the use of non-solid bullets, both used this type of ammunition, in limited quantities. On the right is a C IV hollow-point round, often incorrectly referred to as a 'dum-dum' round. True dum-dum rounds have lead tips.

British Artillery

by MC Heunis

The British Army had several artillery units at its disposal when war broke out. The Royal Horse Artillery's batteries were equipped with light 12-pounder field guns. All its members were mounted, meaning that this unit could keep up with the cavalry.

The Royal Field Artillery, on the other hand, used slightly heavier 15-pounder field guns and 5-inch field howitzers. The crews moved on foot or rode on the ammunition wagons. This made them suited to supporting the slower-moving infantry.

The Royal Garrison Artillery manned the heavy 4.7- and 5-inch garrison and siege guns, as well as the 6-inch howitzers. This unit included a few mountain batteries; their light mountain guns could be broken up into pieces and were then carried by mules. In addition to these imperial units, colonial and volunteer units, including the Natal Field Artillery, Diamond Fields Artillery and City of London Field Battery, manned field guns.

All in all, this formidable artillery force comprised about 750 guns and 20 000 men, yet the Boers still caught the British on the wrong foot when they deployed their four heavy Long Toms in the field. This was before the Royal Garrison Artillery's heavy guns had been shipped in.

British generals were forced, as an interim measure, to mount a range of heavy naval guns from their warships on makeshift wagon and rail chassis for deployment in the field. Sailors found themselves high and dry, servicing 12-pounder, 4.7-inch and 6-inch naval guns deep within the interior.

When the Royal Garrison Artillery landed, preparations for the long-awaited Pretoria fort bombardment got under way. Two enormous 9.45-inch mortars were imported from Austria, and a huge 9.2-inch gun from a Cape fort was mounted on a train carriage. The heavy artillery and its ammunition was hauled to Pretoria with substantial effort, in vain: the guns of the forts were no longer in place when the British reached Pretoria.

A British observation balloon at Modderspruit in Natal. The use of balloons allowed the Royal Artillery to calculate range accurately during the bombardment, for example, of General Piet Cronjé's force at Paardeberg.

This 5-inch Mark IV breech-loading cannon, one of 18 used by the Royal Garrison Artillery during the war, can be found on the premises of the War Museum in Bloemfontein. It is mounted on the chassis of an older, 40-pounder muzzle-loading gun. This gun was extremely accurate at 7 000 paces and reasonably accurate at 8 500 paces. It could fire as far as 11 000 paces, however, trumping the Long Tom's range. But, the 5-inch projectiles were only half the size of the Long Tom's.

In numbers alone, British field artillery outweighed that of the Boers. British strategy fell short, however, and the guns were often inappropriately used. For example, the Boers plundered several field guns at Colenso after the British deployed them too near to Boer lines. In addition, British field artillery used shrapnel, which had a far shorter range than ordinary shells. It soon became clear to the British, too, that lyddite – the latest high-explosive propellant for heavy-calibre ammunition – was not as effective as they had hoped.

All these factors aside, the British gunners persevered. Once their commanders had modified their tactics, they were able to play an important role in winning the war.

LEFT One of about 50 5-inch lyddite projectiles discovered near Senekal in the 1980s. The 5-inch breech-loading gun and the 5-inch field howitzer could fire these projectiles, which were filled with lyddite, a yellow, high-explosive propellant that exploded almost like dynamite. Before the war, the British press trumpeted the potency of lyddite, but the material fell far short of these expectations.

FAR LEFT Men of the Royal Field Artillery with an Armstrong gun.

The Orange Free State Artillery Corps

by MC Heunis

The Orange Free State Artillery Corps (hereafter the Free State Artillery Corps) had existed since 1854, the year in which the Republic of the Orange Free State gained its independence from Britain. It participated in the wars against the Basotho in the 1860s, but only started to take shape in earnest after 1880 when FWR Albrecht, a seasoned Prussian artilleryman, assumed command.

Albrecht's accomplished leadership saw the corps develop systematically. The men were schooled in strict German principles, and fitted out with equipment and uniforms from Germany. Ceremonial dress, for example, consisted of a blue jacket with orange trim in the German style, worn with leather spiked helmets (*Pickelhauben*) or caps and German swords. Field uniforms were made of brown corduroy fabric and had black trim. They were worn with German-style forage caps and short swords.

Buildings in and around Fort Bloemfontein housed the corps, which numbered five officers and 159 soldiers and non-commissioned officers at the time of the war. Reservists pushed this number to 400. The corps had a well-trained heliograph and signalling division, to which Gideon Scheepers belonged. (Scheepers later led a commando into the Cape Colony and was captured by the British and executed by a military firing squad at Graaff-Reinet.) Well-known sieges and battles in which the corps participated include those at Ladysmith, Kimberley, Stormberg, Modder River, Magersfontein, Spioenkop, Vaalkrans and Paardeberg.

The Free State Artillery Corps' arsenal boasted 14 75-mm Krupp breech-loading guns, five 9-pounder Armstrong muzzle-loading guns, one 37-mm Krupp-Gruson rapid-fire gun, three 3-pounder Whitworth muzzle-loading mountain guns and three Martini-Henry Maxim machine guns.

The 37-mm rapid-fire gun aside, all the artillery still used black powder. This rendered them somewhat out of date, as a conspicuous cloud of white smoke was produced every time the guns were fired – clearly signposting their position to the enemy. As a result, the corps had to move the location of its guns frequently during battle.

Albrecht and a number of artillerymen, with three guns, were forced to surrender with General Piet Cronjé at Paardeberg, but the

Helmets like this one – called a *Pickelhaube*, German for 'spiked hat' – were only worn for parades and special occasions at the barracks, and not in the field. Horse hair, shown here, replaced the ball at the top of the helmet for formal parades. This helmet belonged to Lieutenant Johan du Toit Böning, who commanded the Free State's guns on the Natal front.

The ceremonial dress of the Free State Artillery Corps, pictured here, closely resembled that of the Prussian Guard artillery regiment, Major FWR Albrecht's old unit, although it had orange trim instead of red. The white leather belt's copper buckle and the black leather tas worn on the white shoulder strap were both embellished in copper with the Orange Free State coat of arms.

remaining corps members and guns continued to serve with the commandos well into the war. They frequently used guns plundered from the British to supplement their diminished resources, and played a significant role in helping to keep President MT Steyn and General Christiaan de Wet out of British hands during their raids.

When ammunition for their guns eventually ran out or fell into British hands, the surviving artillerymen fought as ordinary burghers to the bitter end.

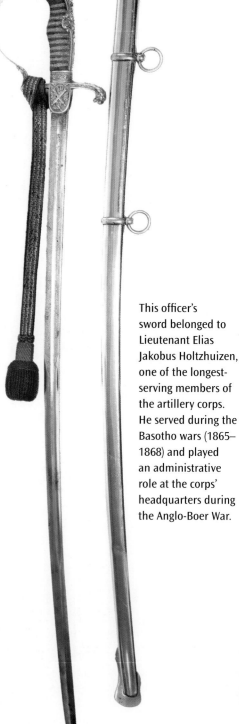

This officer's sword belonged to Lieutenant Elias Jakobus Holtzhuizen, one of the longest-serving members of the artillery corps. He served during the Basotho wars (1865–1868) and played an administrative role at the corps' headquarters during the Anglo-Boer War.

Soldiers and officers of the Free State Artillery Corps, and two Krupp field guns, in the Fort Bloemfontein courtyard. Sergeant Gideon Scheepers is second from left in the front.

The Transvaal State Artillery

by MC Heunis

The Transvaal State Artillery dates back to the founding of Batterij Dingaan, the republic's first formal artillery unit, in 1874. This unit was dissolved in 1877, when Britain annexed the Transvaal, however, but was reformed after the First War of Independence, in 1881. It was part of the police force for a time, before becoming the State Artillery of the South African Republic in 1894.

After the Jameson Raid of 1895–1896, the government bolstered the State Artillery: it imported guns, built forts in Pretoria and Johannesburg, and laid out a substantial, modern artillery camp in Pretoria. The unit comprised three field batteries, a garrison artillery corps to man the forts, a mountain artillery unit, a field telegraph division, medical services, a band and an army service corps.

Members of the State Artillery by 7-pounder guns seized at Kraaipan.

State Artillery ceremonial dress borrowed from Austrian and Dutch designs: dark-blue atilla jackets with black trim were worn with white pith helmets or fur busbies (unit-dependent) and British or German swords. (The atilla jacket is a decorative cavalry coat of Hungarian origin, embellished with buttons and piping.) Sand-coloured Bedford cord field uniforms were worn with Austrian caps or felt hats. The drab colours of their uniforms earned members of the State Artillery the nickname 'Oom Paul se vales' (Uncle Paul's drab ones).

By October 1899, the State Artillery had grown to 17 officers and 633 soldiers. It was reorganised when war broke out; most of its men and guns were deployed on the four fronts, as both field and siege artillery, and they became a redoubtable force. The four 155-mm Long Toms, in particular, quickly became infamous, inspiring awe in many a British soldier.

The State Artillery's practice of camouflaging and concealing its guns had a lasting impression on artillery tactics. It was also one of the first units in the world to use indirect fire: when the target was not in direct line of sight, the gun was ranged using aiming posts, heliographs or flag signals. This technique was successfully deployed at Spioenkop, Tugela Heights and at Bergendal.

Once the sieges of Ladysmith, Mafeking and Kimberley had been relieved, the State Artillery continued to fight until dwindling ammunition supplies compelled the men to destroy their guns in the eastern Transvaal and throw them into rivers. The soldiers who remained fought on as ordinary citizens.

The corduroy field uniform worn by State Artilleryman Klopper during the war. These jackets did not last long in the field; Klopper's is one of only two surviving examples.

A member of the State Artillery in his field uniform, 1890s.

Members of the
State Artillery
in their parade
uniforms. Note the
atilla jackets and
fur caps.

State Artillery officers' ceremonial dress included
a shoulder strap and leather pouch with gilded
copper embellishments – including an officers'
whistle tethered to the strap with a fine chain.
Originally used to hold stationery for written reports
and, later, ammunition for the officer's pistol,
the pouches were for ceremonial use only.

The Long Tom

by MC Heunis

Surely the most famous gun of the Anglo-Boer War, the Long Tom became an internationally recognised symbol of Boer resistance.

Four heavy Long Toms – or, rather, 155-mm Model 1877 Long System Schneider-Creusot breech-loading siege guns – were ordered in 1896–1897 to be mounted in the four forts being built around Pretoria: this was a mistake, strictly speaking, since the Long Toms, mounted on wheels, were siege guns and not garrison guns. When war broke out, however, this mistake counted in the Boers' favour: their guns may have been too heavy to be used as ordinary field artillery, but the Boers still succeeded in mounting them in the unlikeliest of positions, thanks to a team of 20 oxen and plenty of manpower, ropes, chains, spades and picks.

The Long Toms were a thorn in British flesh from the outset. With a range of 7 500 to 11 000 m, they far outranged any British artillery in South Africa at the time. Their 43-kg projectiles were also a great shock to the British high command, who were under the impression that all the Boers' heavy artillery was securely mounted in Pretoria. It was a Long Tom that convinced the enemy to evacuate Dundee in Natal, despite the British having won the Battle of Talana, and a Long Tom that, likewise, contributed to the Boer victory at Modderspruit.

During the sieges of Ladysmith, Mafeking and Kimberley, the use of Long Toms forced the British high command to mount heavy naval guns on makeshift chassis and send them to the interior. One of the Long Toms was damaged in a night raid outside Ladysmith, but the gun was returned to Pretoria where the damaged section of its barrel was cut off. Brought back into service, it was moved to Kimberley to lend its might to the besieging Boer forces there.

The Long Toms were put to effective use even after the British had relieved the sieges: the four guns were taken back with the Boers to the eastern Transvaal, to be reunited in August 1900 at the Battle of Bergendal. This was the only battle in which all four guns were used together.

The Transvalers resorted to guerrilla warfare after Bergendal. The heavy Long Toms were not nimble enough to follow, and had, besides, all but run out of ammunition. One gun was dispatched by train to Komatipoort; two others were hauled over what would later become known as the Long Tom Pass, the British hot on their heels.

When these warhorses' ammunition eventually ran out, and the inevitability of their falling into enemy hands became clear, their crews destroyed each one with dynamite.

The original Dutch handbook for the Long Tom gun, containing a description of all the component parts, maintenance instructions, the firing drill, ammunition information, lists of tools and accessories, and scale drawings of the gun, chassis and equipment.

Fort Daspoort's Long Tom gun in action during the siege of Mafeking. The South African Republic imported the weapons in 1896 to arm Pretoria's four forts. After the war broke out, however, the guns were deployed in the field, notably during the sieges of Kimberley, Ladysmith and Mafeking. *Western Cape Archives*

This 155-mm Long Tom shell, excavated in 1941, was likely buried near Dalmanutha in August 1900 during the Battle of Bergendal, where all four Long Toms were used simultaneously. 🔫

Two British doctors and their nursing staff with their Boer helpers, who can be recognised by their *kappies*. Many young Boer women worked as trainee nurses in the concentration camp hospitals.

CHAPTER 5

Medical Services

The Royal Army Medical Corps

When the Anglo-Boer War broke out in 1899, British military authorities believed it would be over by early 1900. The Royal Army Medical Corps, having formally come into being only about a year earlier, was unprepared for a war that would last nearly three years: in the end, more British soldiers would die as a result of illness and other secondary causes than on the battlefield.

Shortly after the Crimean War (1853–1856), the military command started to operationalise better-organised medical care for its soldiers. In the 19th century, however, medical care was still in its infancy. In 1898, the newly formed Royal Army Medical Corps ranked low in the military hierarchy, and endured manpower and equipment shortages.

Medical care on the Anglo-Boer War battlefield was reasonably well organised, nonetheless. On the Natal front, in the war's first four months, Indian stretcher-bearers ferried the wounded from the battlefield to emergency aid posts. The critically injured were taken to Durban on hospital trains and, if necessary, home to Britain by ship.

A range of organisations and prominent figures from the British gentry helped to rope in hospital ships such as the *Maine* and trains such as the *Princess Christian's Red Cross*. Their efforts also rallied into service the Portland and Langman field hospitals in Bloemfontein, and the Imperial

This garrison hospital was erected on the grounds of Fort Bloemfontein after the outbreak of the dysentery epidemic. The shortage of hospital beds for the troops was so dire that several prefabricated buildings destined for Burma (now Myanmar) were diverted to South Africa in 1900. After the war, the building served as a weaving school for Emily Hobhouse's pupils. It was rescued from demolition in 2011 and relocated to the grounds of the War Museum.

Dr Thresh's Current Steam Disinfectant Machine, designed in 1894 for British army and naval use, was intended to disinfect and delouse uniforms. It stands on the premises of the War Museum.

'Soon some 9 000 troops were infected with cholera, which culminated in dysentery on an epidemic scale. The Army was not prepared for an outbreak of disease on such a large scale and sick troops were laid on blankets and tattered ground sheets in inches of mud, sardined so tightly that it was hard to move amongst them … At Bloemfontein alone as many as fifty men died in one day, and more than 1 000 new graves in the cemetery testify to the severity of the epidemic. For more than two months the hospitals were choked with sick.'
– Arthur Conan Doyle on conditions in Bloemfontein, from *The Great Boer War*.

Yeomanry Hospital at Deelfontein near De Aar, in the Cape Colony.

The lack of sizeable hospitals and decent infrastructure made the western front more of a problem, especially after the battles of Belmont, Graspan, Modder River, Magersfontein and Paardeberg, where thousands of soldiers were wounded. The railway line did help to evacuate casualties quickly to hospitals, however.

Medical care improved after the fall of the republican capitals, as critical infrastructure became available: some rural church buildings

ABOVE British military authorities turned the building of Grey College in Bloemfontein into a hospital when a dysentery epidemic broke out among British soldiers.

BELOW British wounded are evacuated by train to hospitals in Cape Town.

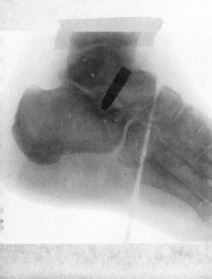

X-rays: a recent innovation

This X-ray from the Anglo-Boer War is one of a handful that has been preserved. Taken by the British medical services, it shows the foot of one burgher Viljoen – and the bullet that is clearly lodged inside it.

In 1896, William Röntgen made the X-ray known to the world. When war broke out, the Volkshospitaal in Pretoria and the Johannesburg Hospital already had X-ray machines. Shortly before the war, Dr WJ Leyds, the Transvaal's envoy in Europe, had ordered three X-ray machines from German manufacturer Siemens & Halske. The machines were labelled 'military equipment' in Delagoa Bay harbour, however, and seized. After the war, they were sent back to Siemens & Halske.

The Bloemfontein cemetery, and the graves of the scores of British soldiers lost to the dysentery epidemic that broke out shortly after Lord Roberts's occupation of Bloemfontein. *Free State Archive*

were repurposed as hospitals, as was the newly completed Palace of Justice in Pretoria. Nurses to staff these were recruited from across the British Empire.

After the British victory at Paardeberg at the end of February 1900, and subsequent battles at Poplar Grove and Abrahamskraal, a nearly 34 000-strong British force occupied Bloemfontein – the culmination of a march that had advanced at a rate of 40 km per day in extreme summer heat and thunderstorms, over treacherously muddy roads.

The troops suffered desperate exhaustion. In the Paardeberg heat, they had not only drunk contaminated water from the Modder River but had also filled their water carts with it for the long march to Bloemfontein. They stood little chance against the dysentery epidemic that swept through the Bloemfontein camp, killing hundreds.

An Australian soldier described the wretchedness of the war's biggest medical challenge in his diary: 'March 15 – Raining night and day, camp ankle deep in slush. Sickness increasing fast. Dysentery and cramps … Enteric fever now breaking out badly in regiment.'

Bloemfontein was simply not equipped for the huge influx of soldiers. It did not take long for the town's fresh water to run out; old wells were reopened, whose water was 'simply alive with a moving wriggling mass of putridity'. The overloaded sewerage system could not cope. By the time the dysentery epidemic had finally been brought under control, about 1 900 British troops had been buried between March and April 1900 – many in mass graves in the Bloemfontein cemetery.

The war was important schooling for the Royal Army Medical Corps. A monument in Aldershot, England, erected in 1905, memorialises the corps' contribution as well as the lives of over 300 of its members who died in the war. Five members of the unit were awarded the Victoria Cross.

Mohandas Karamchand Gandhi (circled) and the Indian Bearer Corps.

The Natal Volunteer Ambulance Corps and the Indian Bearer Corps

At the start of the war, the Royal Army Medical Corps enlisted 1 000 Indian men to transport the wounded from battlefields to emergency aid posts. This group of stretcher-bearers was known as the Natal Volunteer Ambulance Corps.

The unit quickly grew to 1 800 members, divided into four companies. Each company was split, in turn, into divisions of 25 men each. The corps, which rendered invaluable service at Colenso, Spioenkop, Vaalkrans and Pietershoogte, was disbanded after the relief of Ladysmith, to be replaced by the Imperial Bearer Corps.

The lawyer and future political leader Mohandas Karamchand Gandhi (later known as Mahatma), who was secretary of the Indian Congress in Natal at the time, created the Indian Bearer Corps early in the war. The corps was a volunteer unit of about 100 men. As a British subject, Gandhi sought to remain loyal to the Crown, but also believed that the republics' fight was justified. He served, therefore, on condition that none of his volunteers were to be deployed in an armed capacity.

Dr LP Booth, a missionary with a military background, gave the volunteers basic training. Natal's colonial government initially spurned the Indian Bearer Corps' offer of voluntary help; after the British suffered a series of defeats, however, it quickly changed its tune.

The first bearer unit, stationed at Estcourt, reached the front in mid-December 1899 – just in time for the aftermath of the Battle of Colenso. The Natal Volunteer Ambulance Corps had already removed the badly wounded from the battlefield and taken them to medical aid posts. Members of the Indian Bearer Corps ferried these casualties on the next leg of their journey, to railway stations such as Frere and Chieveley. From there, the casualties were sent on to hospitals.

The unit's diligence earned its members the respect of both friend and foe; they are remembered particularly for their duties after the Battle of Spioenkop.

In February 1900, after just six weeks, the Natal Volunteer Ambulance Corps was disbanded. The Crown seemed quickly to forget about the contribution that the Indian stretcher-bearers had made. They received only bronze Queen's South Africa medals, not silver ones; Queen Victoria's Christmas gift, a tin of chocolate given to all troops in South Africa, was not extended to these Indian volunteers. Gandhi responded by raising an objection with British military authorities.

The contribution of Indian South Africans to the Anglo-Boer War was initially recognised only by bronze Queen's South Africa medals, while regular British soldiers received the medal in silver. This was later rectified. This Queen's South Africa medal (silver) was awarded to Mani Kum Royeppen, leader of the Natal Volunteer Ambulance Corps.

Medical Services in the Republics

Medical services in the two Boer republics were still very basic when war broke out. Most doctors were trained abroad, and were of European descent. With the exception of the hospitals in Johannesburg and Pretoria, most hospitals – such as those in Barberton, Klerksdorp, Krugersdorp, Haenertsburg and Potchefstroom – offered only limited services. Bloemfontein's Volkshospitaal and the St George's Cottage Hospital were the Orange Free State's only reputable medical facilities.

The Boer republics also lacked an extended ambulance service. The Transvaalsche Roode Kruis, also known as the Pretoria Ambulance Corps, was established only in 1896, and was poorly organised. Nurses were trained in only the most basic medical support. In the Orange Free State, the Oranje Vrijstaat Ambulans acted as a Red Cross unit. The republics imported most medical equipment and supplies.

When the war began, some local Transvaal companies found themselves roped into providing medical supplies. For example, the workshops of the Nederlandsch-Zuid-Afrikaansche Spoorweg- maatschappij (Netherlands-South African Railway Company, or NZASM) transformed railway carriages into three mobile railway ambulances. Each train comprised two hospital carriages, a kitchen and a supply carriage. Two of these 'flying ambulances' served on the Natal front; the third served between Bloemfontein and Pretoria.

In the war's guerrilla phase, Boer fighters' access to formal medical services gradually dissipated. The burghers fell back on the care of women refugees, or of women who had not yet fled their farms. They plundered medical supplies from British supply columns whenever they could.

A Transvaal ambulance train, one of three trains that were customised for use during the war. The train was initially manned by the Transvaalsche Roode Kruis; the Eerste Nederlandse Ambulans later constituted most of the 'flying ambulance' staff.

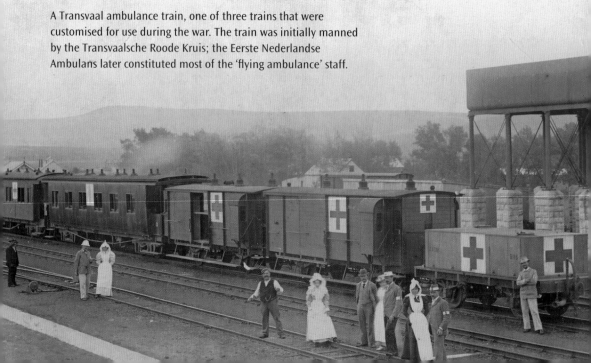

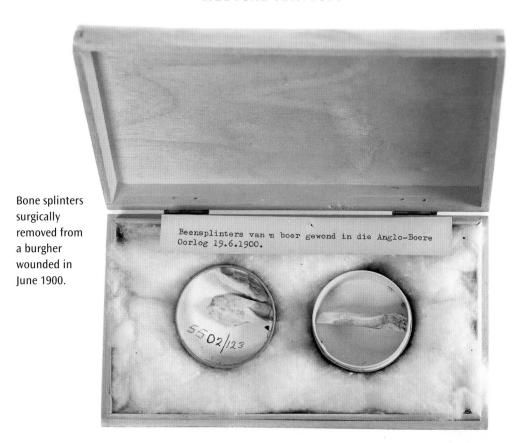

Bone splinters surgically removed from a burgher wounded in June 1900.

Beensplinters van n boer gewond in die Anglo-Boere Oorlog 19.6.1900.

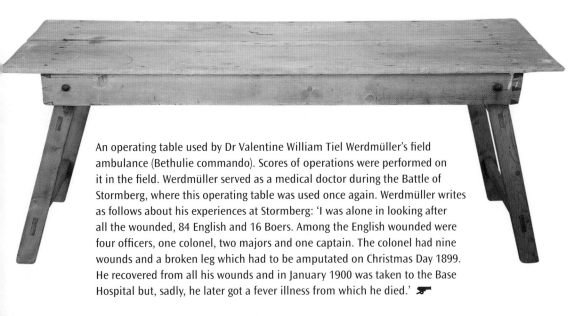

An operating table used by Dr Valentine William Tiel Werdmüller's field ambulance (Bethulie commando). Scores of operations were performed on it in the field. Werdmüller served as a medical doctor during the Battle of Stormberg, where this operating table was used once again. Werdmüller writes as follows about his experiences at Stormberg: 'I was alone in looking after all the wounded, 84 English and 16 Boers. Among the English wounded were four officers, one colonel, two majors and one captain. The colonel had nine wounds and a broken leg which had to be amputated on Christmas Day 1899. He recovered from all his wounds and in January 1900 was taken to the Base Hospital but, sadly, he later got a fever illness from which he died.'

The hat worn by an orderly of
the Pretoria Ambulance Corps.

Help from Afar for the Republics

The nations of Europe may have been reluctant to become embroiled in the war, but many of their populations were sympathetic to the Boer cause. The decision was made to muster an ambulance service, under the banner of the International Red Cross, to give medical support to republican forces.

After making landfall at Delagoa Bay, several ambulance services reached Pretoria between December 1899 and April 1900. They provided medical services in the field and in the towns during the war's first phase.

The Netherlands, for example, sent two fully equipped ambulances. The Eerste Nederlandse Ambulans set up a hospital in Pretoria's Staatsmeisieskool (State Girls' School), while others served on one of the Red Cross hospital trains. The Holland Transvaal Association of Detroit, in the United States, collected funds for the wounded, and for widows and orphans.

The Tsarina of Russia supplied an ambulance of doctors, nine nurses and 12 male orderlies. In Natal, the Russians established hospitals at Glencoe and Newcastle; the French contributed two fully equipped field hospitals.

Ambulance services came from as far afield as Germany, Belgium, Switzerland, the Scandinavian countries and Dutch East India. Two ambulance units of the German Red Cross served in the Orange Free State, at Jacobsdal, Brandfort,

The Nederlandse Ambulans (Dutch ambulance) at Modderspruit farm, outside Ladysmith, in Natal. The Battle of Modderspruit on 30 October 1899 was a victory for republican forces.

Norvalspont, Kroonstad, Heilbron, Bethlehem and Fouriesburg.

The dozens of nurses who served with the local and foreign ambulance services attracted much attention. The belief that the women were in South Africa only for 'een plezier tochtje' (a little adventure) made the more conservative elements of Boer society regard them, initially, with great suspicion.

A Jewish organisation in Johannesburg – the Chevra Kadisha, or Jewish Helping Hand – pitched in by setting up a hospital in a Johannesburg cigar factory. This local organisation also received funds from abroad.

When the Boer capitals fell to the British army, most foreign ambulances left South Africa, although some doctors did remain to serve the commandos.

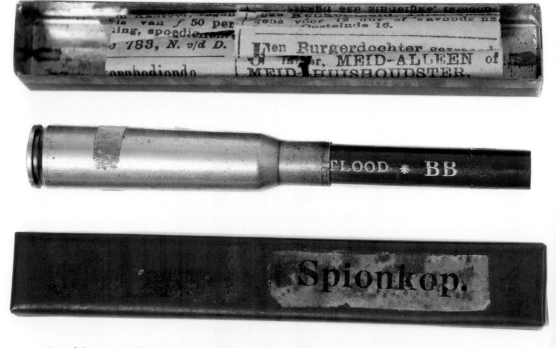

One of the 500 pencils made in aid of the Dutch Red Cross. The pencils were sold in the Netherlands to raise funds for the Dutch Red Cross ambulance, which served in the republics. 🔫

This instrument pouch belonged to Nurse J de Wit van der Hoop of the Tweede Nederlandse Ambulans, which was stationed at Christiana, among other locations. The pouch holds six different medical instruments. ⌐

The British humanist Emily Hobhouse, who played a major role
in the war, made several watercolour paintings during her visits
to South Africa. This painting is of the burned-down homestead
on General Christiaan de Wet's farm Rooipoort.

CHAPTER 6

The War's Cast of Characters

Paul Kruger

Stephanus Johannes Paulus Kruger was born on 10 October 1825 in the Cradock district, on the eastern border of the Cape Colony. He made the Great Trek to the north as a young boy along with the Voortrekkers; his family settled in the Potchefstroom area. In 1842, at the age of 16, he was granted the farm Waterkloof, in the Rustenburg district.

Kruger played a significant role in the Transvaal's pioneer era, distinguishing himself as a skilled military man and politician. He was present at the signing of the Sand River Convention with Britain, in 1852 – marking the birth of the South African Republic. Time and again, his military leadership came to the fore in the numerous conflicts with indigenous peoples within the Transvaal's borders and in the First War of Independence (1880–1881).

Kruger's worldview was firmly grounded in the Bible; his unwavering Christian faith made him a favourite among his people. When the new Raadsaal was erected in Pretoria, he took exception to the fact that the head of the female figure on the dome was uncovered. The young woman could not, according to the old president, stand there, in the Transvaal wind and rain, without a hat; a helmet was promptly made for the statue.

Kruger was elected president of the South African Republic in 1883. He endeavoured to keep the Transvaal beyond Britain's sphere of influence, but the discovery of gold on the Witwatersrand increased the tension between the two governments. One of the reasons for this tension was the question of suffrage for the thousands of foreigners – termed 'Uitlanders' – who descended upon the gold fields to work. In 1890, Kruger increased the residency period for voting rights from seven to 14 years.

On the eve of the Anglo-Boer War, Kruger made it clear at the Bloemfontein Conference (31 May to 5 June 1899) that he was prepared to make concessions – including returning to a residency period of seven years. Sir Alfred Milner then insisted on a five-year period. Kruger was certain that an honourable agreement with Britain was no longer possible.

The South African Republic and Orange Free State handed an ultimatum to Britain on 9 October 1899. The ultimatum, which mentioned the build-up of British troops on the borders of the republics, among other issues, was rejected. Two days later, war broke out.

Despite his poor health and advanced years, 74-year-old Kruger kept his burghers' spirits high through wise advice, telegraph messages and even personal visits to the Natal and western Free State fronts. When the march of the British forces on Pretoria began to appear unstoppable, Kruger and the Volksraad moved the seat of government to the eastern Transvaal on 29 May 1900.

A brass plate affixed to the bow of the Dutch cruiser *Gelderland* for Kruger's passage to Europe. The ship departed Lourenço Marques on 20 October 1900.

It was decided, shortly afterwards, to send Kruger to Europe via Lourenço Marques. There, he would try to convince European nations to take up arms in the republican fight. Queen Wilhelmina of the Netherlands dispatched the cruiser *Gelderland* to fetch him. Though he received a hero's welcome, with European statesmen lavishing sympathy upon him, Kruger quickly realised that he would not be able to rely on Europe for military or diplomatic support.

He lived his last days alone in exile in Clarens, Switzerland, where he passed away on 14 July 1904. He was laid to rest in Pretoria's Ou Kerkhof on 16 December 1904.

Artist Erich Mayer's portrait of Paul Kruger, painted while Mayer was a prisoner of war on St Helena. Mayer also painted a portrait of Orange Free State president MT Steyn while on the island. In a letter accompanying his two artworks, Mayer explained: 'I painted President Kruger from a sketch that appeared in a Swiss newspaper that I obtained. However, I was not very happy with the painting … because his complexion was too dull. I used a fellow prisoner of war, who resembled the president closely, as a model and repainted the painting. Many of the prisoners of war got tears in their eyes on viewing the finished product. The fine cracks in the portrait are a result of the fact that, on my return to South Africa, I rolled it up to save space in my luggage.' There are ten pieces by Mayer in the War Museum's art collection. 🔫

MT Steyn

Marthinus Theunis Steyn was the first president of the Republic of the Orange Free State who was born a Free Stater. He was born on 2 October 1857 on a farm outside Winburg and educated at Grey College in Bloemfontein.

He was admitted to the esteemed Honourable Society of the Inner Temple in London in January 1880, where he trained as an advocate, and gained admission to the Bar in 1882. He opened a legal practice in Bloemfontein on his return, and married Rachel Isabella (Tibbie) Fraser, daughter of a Philippolis minister, in 1883.

Steyn was appointed attorney general and, later, criminal lawyer, of the Orange Free State in 1887. In 1895, he was elected as the republic's sixth president; during his term he endeavoured to win the loyalty and political cooperation of English-speaking Free Staters. He arranged the Bloemfontein Conference in May 1889 in an attempt to bridge the divide between Paul Kruger's South African Republic and Sir Alfred Milner, governor of the Cape Colony and British high commissioner for South Africa.

The failure of the conference notwithstanding, Steyn persisted, through tireless diplomatic negotiations with both parties, in trying to avoid war. He had no choice, ultimately, but to honour his allegiance to the South African Republic. According to Karel Schoeman's *Bloemfontein, die ontstaan van 'n stad 1846–1946*, Steyn declared to the Free State Volksraad on 22 September 1899 that he would 'rather lose the independence of the Orange Free State honourably than preserve it dishonourably or through infidelity'.

Steyn was the 'soul of the struggle' during the war, often visiting the commandos to boost the morale of the burghers. He was elected for a second presidential term in 1900.

When Bloemfontein fell, the Orange Free State government became a government at large, with General Christiaan de Wet's commando as its escort. In 1901, Steyn was with the Free State forces in Reitz when British troops almost seized him in a surprise early-morning attack. Steyn escaped, thanks to Jan Ruiter, his vigilant *agterryer*, or groom (see the following page).

In the closing months of the war, Steyn's health started to fail. He continued to insist, however, that peace would only be possible if the Boers could retain their independence. In January 1902, the Dutch government sent a note to the British government offering mediation. Lord Kitchener forwarded the note to acting president Schalk Burger. As a result, 60 representatives of the two republics met in April to discuss continuing the war and Britain's suggestions for peace. A month later, a delegation of leaders from the two republics met in Vereeniging to discuss Britain's peace proposals further and to negotiate with the British government.

Suffering partial paralysis due to illness, Steyn could not participate actively in the talks. He resigned as president on 29 May; De Wet was appointed acting president. So it was that when peace was concluded, Steyn had remained true to his resolution never to sign a document that gave away the republic's independence.

The scarf that
President
MT Steyn wore
during his escape
from Reitz.

Steyn (circled) on commando, probably at Kroonstad. To his right
is Abraham Fischer, who chaired the Bloemfontein Conference.

Jan Ruiter and Other Agterryers (Grooms)

Orange Free State commando law ruled that black men could also be called up for commando service. About 12 000 grooms were thought to have gone on commando. When war broke out, many Boers in the two republics took trusted farm workers with them on commando as grooms.

The groom's primary role was logistical: caring for horses, gathering firewood, boiling water, cooking food and putting up tents. While not a common occurrence, some grooms went into combat; a few perished in this way.

Griqua groom Jan Ruiter, President MT Steyn's groom, was very well known. In July 1901, the Orange Free State government found itself temporarily seated in the little town of Reitz. On the morning of 11 July, a British force under General RG Broadwood surrounded the town.

Colonel John Blake, an Irish-American volunteer with the Irish Volunteers on the Boer side, and his groom.

COLONEL BLAKE
IRISH BRIGADE

With the enemy approaching, Ruiter immediately roused the president and helped him to escape on his horse, Scot. He went on to convince the British soldier who wanted to give chase that the president was just an old farmer not worth catching. A substantial contingent of the Orange Free State government – officials, part of the government archives and the republic's gold reserves, including 800 gold pounds – were not so lucky and fell into British hands.

The British released all grooms in the government's retinue shortly after the incident, and Ruiter managed to rejoin the president. He lived out the rest of his days on Onze Rust, the president's farm outside Bloemfontein, and was laid to rest there after his death.

Willem Snowball, Commandant CTM Willcocks's groom. Snowball was exiled, with Willcocks, as a prisoner of war to Diyatalawa in Ceylon (now Sri Lanka).

Jan Ruiter, President Steyn's loyal groom.

Christiaan de Wet

Celebrated soldier Christiaan Rudolf de Wet was born on 7 October 1854, the same year as the Republic of the Orange Free State came into being. He was a born soldier, and was all of 11 years of age when he joined a commando that patrolled the Free State border during one of the Basotho wars.

Christiaan and his brother fought in the battles at Laing's Nek, Ingogo and Majuba during the First War of Independence (1880–1881). His strong leadership qualities saw him elected as a member of the Free State Volksraad from 1889 to 1898. The Jameson Raid made him a vehement supporter of MT Steyn's policy of closer cooperation with the South African Republic.

At the outbreak of the Anglo-Boer War, the 45-year-old De Wet was a member of the Heilbron commando and fought, at his sons' side, in several of the battles in Natal. As acting commandant of the Heilbron commando, he and his 300 men took Nicholson's Nek – and 800 prisoners of war – on 30 November 1899.

The legendary horse Fleur, which bore General Christiaan de Wet through countless dangers.

De Wet's promotion to field general of the Free State forces on 7 December 1899 rewarded his military acumen. At the Battle of Paardeberg, he tried in vain to convince General Piet Cronjé to break out of the ring of British troops encircling his position.

The war's second phase – the guerrilla phase – began with the fall of the two republican capitals. De Wet's military successes and ability to evade British forces earned him international renown during this phase. He defeated the British at Sannaspos (31 March 1900) and Mostertshoek (3 April 1900).

De Wet quickly became a thorn in the side of the British army. Elected as chief commandant of the Free State military, he was the prime target of many a British column's protracted raids. These raids sought to round up De Wet and his government; none ever succeeded.

De Wet's fearlessness inspired not only his burghers but also the women and children in the concentration camps. His brother, Piet, was a sore point, however: after this former Boer general had laid down his weapon, he shifted his allegiance to Britain and joined Kitchener's Burgher Peace Committees. Piet de Wet later also led the Heilbron section of the Orange River Colony Volunteers, a 'joiners' division of the British forces.

De Wet and other guerrilla fighters fought hard, but their war was not to be won. At the talks in Vereeniging, General Louis Botha and General Koos de la Rey convinced De Wet to accept Britain's terms. He left with Botha and De la Rey for Europe to raise funds for impoverished Afrikaners, writing his war memoir during the passage by sea. The memoir was published that same year as *De strijd tusschen Boer en Brit*. An English version (*Three Years' War*) was released immediately, as were translations in several other languages, including Russian.

De Wet is also known for his part in the 1914 Afrikaner rebellion, sparked by the decision of the Union of South Africa to support Britain in the First World War. He was sentenced to imprisonment for his role in the rebellion.

General Christiaan de Wet's saddle, on which he spent the better part of the war. He gave this saddle to one burgher Bester, who had lost his saddle and bridle in a skirmish at Senekal.

A portrait of De Wet by Dutch artist Therese van Duyl-Schwartze. It was never completed: an impatient De Wet could not sit still for more than two sessions. Dr HD van Broekhuizen, a veteran and the erstwhile Union envoy in the Netherlands, bought the portrait from the artist years later.

Louis Botha

Louis Botha was 37 when he rode, as an ordinary burgher, with the Vryheid commando to the Natal border at the onset of war. The extraordinary military skill that he demonstrated in several battles accelerated his rise to the rank of general.

He notched up one of the war's most famous Boer victories on 15 December 1899 when he defeated General Redvers Buller at Colenso. His reputation as a soldier and leader grew at Spioenkop on 24 January 1900.

His appointment as commandant general of the Transvaal forces filled the void that followed General Piet Joubert's death in March of that same year. The war had been in its guerrilla phase for about a year when he met Lord Kitchener at Middelburg in February 1901. There, he rejected the peace proposals that Kitchener presented. The war continued.

In May 1902, Botha acknowledged that victory had slipped beyond the Boers' grasp, and applied himself to securing an honourable peace. He was part of the group that went, with General Christiaan de Wet and General Koos de la Rey, to Europe to raise money to relieve impoverished Afrikaners.

He mobilised Afrikaners in the Transvaal soon after the war, and formed the Het Volk party. This marked the beginning of the Afrikaner's political reawakening. Botha was elected prime minister of the Transvaal Colony in 1907.

Botha became the prime minister of the newly founded Union of South Africa on 31 May 1910. His decision to enter the First World War on the side of Britain culminated in the 1914 Rebellion, led by former Boer generals such as Christiaan de Wet and Christiaan Beyers. Botha's use of military force to oppose the rebellion cost him the support of much of the Afrikaner community.

Botha signed the Treaty of Versailles, which ended the First World War, under protest, believing that its terms sowed the seeds of future conflict.

A riding whip with an ivory handle, used by Commandant General Louis Botha during the war. Like General De Wet with Fleur and Dapper, Botha had two horses – Dapper and Bles.

'I sincerely regret to see that the determination of me and my burghers to persevere in the strike of our independence will be avenged by you on our wives and children.'
– Louis Botha, in a letter to Lord Roberts after the latter had issued a proclamation in September 1900 that the scorched-earth policy would be implemented even more strictly, *The Boer Fight for Freedom*

To raise funds for the many thousands of people whom the war had left in poverty, Generals Louis Botha, Christiaan de Wet and Koos de la Rey departed for Europe on 30 July 1902. Several prominent artists painted their portraits during their stay. This painting, by the respected portraitist Antoon van Welie, who had painted, among others, Dutch royalty, shows Botha suffering the effects of an illness.

Koos de la Rey

A chain of distinction that General Koos de la Rey gave to his military secretary, Ignatius Ferreira.

As a young man, Jacobus Hercules (Koos) de la Rey had seen conflict with indigenous groups, and had also been a combatant in the First War of Independence (1880–1881). He farmed in the western Transvaal, an area he knew so well that he could act as surveyor there as well.

As a prominent farmer and political leader, De la Rey was a member of the Volksraad when the war broke out. He became field general and advisor to General Piet Cronjé. (The stubborn Cronjé's tendency to cling to outmoded military tactics led to frequent differences of opinion between Cronjé and De la Rey.)

It was on De la Rey's order that the first shots of the war were fired, at Kraaipan, southwest of Mafeking, on 12 October 1899. He proved himself a worthy soldier at Modder River by deploying new military tactics early in the conflict. It was at the Battle of Magersfontein, however, that De la Rey distinguished himself as a master tactician; by digging trenches in front of the hills, the Boers positioned themselves exactly where the British least expected to find them.

De la Rey also realised just how important logistical support was to an army as large as Britain's. His proposal to disrupt British supply lines, such as rail connections, was accepted at a war council meeting.

De la Rey's commando was largely autonomous, giving him a great deal of control over the conduct of the war in the western Transvaal. He was appointed western Transvaal assistant commandant general, earning him the honorific 'Lion of the Western Transvaal'. He became a master of mobile warfare by using new tactics, such as storming and surprise attacks. His successes at Silkaatsnek and Nooitgedacht forced the British high command to deploy General Methuen and Colonel Kekewich – both seasoned commanders – in the region. In the last Boer victories of the war, at Ysterspruit and Tweebosch, De la Rey captured Methuen but released him shortly thereafter.

Despite his successes in the war's guerrilla phase, De la Rey had also realised by 1902 that the conflict had become unsustainable. In addition to a fundraising visit to Europe with Generals Christiaan de Wet and Louis Botha, De la Rey went to India in 1903 to try to convince intransigent prisoners of war there to take the British Oath of Neutrality.

De la Rey remained active in South African politics after the war, serving as a senator in the Union parliament. When the First World War broke out, he was among the group of Boer generals who decided to rebel against the Botha government's decision to join the war on Britain's side. In the tense run-up to the rebellion, De la Rey was fatally wounded on 15 September 1914 when the car in which he was travelling sped through a police roadblock and the police opened fire, mistaking the occupants for the fugitive Foster gang.

A charcoal sketch of General Koos de la Rey made in October 1902, shortly after the war.
Dutch artist Therese van Duyl-Schwartze sketched De la Rey during the general's visit to London.

Count de Villebois-Mareuil

Count Georges de Villebois-Mareuil was one of only two foreigners promoted to the rank of general in the republican forces. Georges Henri Anne-Marie Victor de Villebois-Mareuil was a French nobleman, a former French army colonel and a veteran of the Franco-Prussian War (1870–1871).

He arrived in Pretoria in November 1899 to join Boer forces as a foreign volunteer, and was appointed military advisor to Commandant General Joubert, serving in Natal and on the western front. De Villebois-Mareuil led a French volunteer corps in the battles at Abrahamskraal on 10 March. On the same day, General Piet Joubert promoted him to field general. The two Boer presidents ratified this decision at a war council shortly afterwards. Joubert then ordered De Villebois-Mareuil to unify all foreign volunteer units.

The Frenchman described the moment in his war diary as follows: '17 March – Arrived at Kroonstad and found myself in the middle of a war council, to which I was welcomed with the highest honour. The two presidents,

as well as Joubert, stood up and shook my hand. I was offered a seat next to Kruger. They decided to press on with the war ... I was appointed general and received command over all the Europeans, whom I must unite in a legion.'

De Villebois-Mareuil and about 100 men – comprising French and Dutch soldiers and a few Boers – departed for Kimberley on 24 March 1900 to attack British supply lines. On 5 April, Lord Methuen surprised his men, surrounding them near the small town of Boshof. The foreign legion fought valiantly for over four hours, but De Villebois-Mareuil was killed by artillery fire.

In honour of his brave stand – and owing, also, to his aristocratic descent and military background – Lord Methuen ordered De Villebois-Mareuil to be buried at Boshof with full military honours, and paid for the funeral himself. On 14 August 1971, his remains were reinterred in the heroes' acre at Magersfontein.

Lord Chesham, a British officer, sent De Villebois-Mareuil's horse, Colenso, which had been wounded in the battle, to his estate in Buckinghamshire.

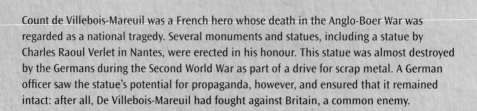

Count de Villebois-Mareuil was a French hero whose death in the Anglo-Boer War was regarded as a national tragedy. Several monuments and statues, including a statue by Charles Raoul Verlet in Nantes, were erected in his honour. This statue was almost destroyed by the Germans during the Second World War as part of a drive for scrap metal. A German officer saw the statue's potential for propaganda, however, and ensured that it remained intact: after all, De Villebois-Mareuil had fought against Britain, a common enemy.

A tile tableau of Count de Villebois-Mareuil, made by the Dutch artist Cornelis de Bruin. In 1900, De Bruin created several such tableaus in recognition of the Boer victories at the start of the war, such as the battles of Stormberg and Magersfontein. The tableaus were erected in the entrance hall of the then newly built Transvalia Theatre in Rotterdam, but were forgotten for many years. In the 1970s, during renovations to the theatre, they were discovered behind wallpaper. Fifteen tableaus were reclaimed and the collection was acquired by the War Museum. 🔫

Lord Roberts

Frederick Sleigh Roberts came from a military family. Despite being blind in his right eye due to 'brain fever', he attended Eton and Sandhurst. The young Lieutenant Roberts soon distinguished himself, making a notable impression during the Indian Mutiny, for which he received the Victoria Cross in 1858.

He went on to serve in the Abyssinian campaigns (1863 and 1867–1868) and in the Second Anglo-Afghan War, distinguishing himself on several occasions. His 480-km relief march from Kabul to Kandahar during the final phase of the Anglo-Afghan War earned him even higher esteem.

Roberts briefly held the position of high commissioner of South Eastern Africa after General George Colley perished in the First War of Independence in the Transvaal. Shortly before his arrival in Cape Town, peace was concluded. He was offered a post in India soon afterwards.

Widely known by the nickname 'Bobs', Roberts was promoted to field marshal in 1895. When the Anglo-Boer War broke out, Sir Redvers Buller was appointed commander in chief, dashing the hopes of the ageing Roberts. The defeats suffered during 'Black Week' damaged Britain's reputation for military prowess, however, and claimed the life of Roberts's only son, Freddie, who died at Colenso.

The Salisbury government replaced Buller with Roberts, who immediately revised British strategy. Under Roberts, the focus shifted to thorough reconnaissance, flanking movements and the use of crossfire and cover. He launched his attack on the republics from the Cape Colony, not from Natal, relieving Kimberley in February 1900. He went on to defeat General Piet Cronjé at Paardeberg and occupy Bloemfontein on 13 March 1900.

The Boer victories at Sannaspos (31 March 1900) and Reddersburg (4 April 1900) aside, Roberts firmly believed that the war would end with the fall of Pretoria. However, the decision of the Boers to adopt guerrilla tactics meant that the war would last another two years.

Roberts responded by issuing proclamations and implementing draconian countermeasures: all Boer homes that were in a certain radius of where guerrilla attacks took place were to be burnt to the ground. He also set up refugee

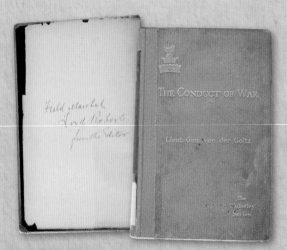

A copy of *The Conduct of War* by Colmar von der Goltz, which belonged to Lord Roberts. The publication was discovered among documents in the Castle of Good Hope, in Cape Town, and donated to the War Museum by a former officer who worked there.

camps for those who wished to seek British protection; these camps were the precursors of the concentration camps.

Roberts continued to believe that the war would end quickly during the guerrilla phase, especially in the wake of the British victories at Brandwater Basin, near Fouriesburg, in July 1900 and at Bergendal in August 1900. On 29 November 1900, he ordered Kitchener, his chief of staff, to extinguish all remaining resistance.

Queen Victoria honoured Roberts by making him an earl, among other gestures. He was appointed Commander in Chief of the Forces, a position he held until 8 February 1904. He remained actively involved in Britain's defence: when the First World War broke out, he was given the position of Colonel in Chief of overseas forces in England, a title he held until his death, at 82, in November 1914.

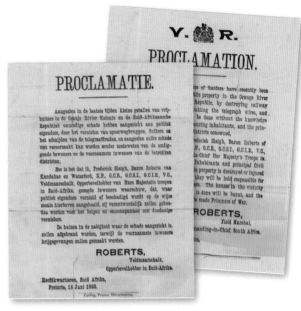

Lord Roberts issued his first proclamation on 16 June 1900, warning citizens of the two republics that property would be razed in areas where the railway line had been sabotaged.

The enormous public interest in the Anglo-Boer War saw numerous war souvenirs being manufactured. This plate, depicting Lord Roberts, shows the high esteem in which Britain's military leaders were held.

Lord Kitchener

Horatio Herbert Kitchener began his military training at the Royal Military Academy in Woolwich, in 1867. Four years later, when the Franco-Prussian War broke out, he joined a French ambulance unit. He held several military positions in the British Empire between 1866 and 1899, mostly in Egypt. As Sirdar – commander of Egyptian military forces – Kitchener enjoyed a high standing in military circles.

Kitchener's military career peaked after his renowned victories over the Mahdists in the battles of Atbara (8 April 1898) and Omdurman (2 September 1898) in the Sudan, and the reoccupation of Khartoum. He was created a baron and appointed governor general of the Sudan.

On Lord Roberts's appointment as commander of British forces in South Africa, Kitchener became Roberts's chief of staff. He failed his first test on South African soil by ordering the attack on Cronjé's camp during the Battle of Paardeberg, on 18 February 1900. The day's British losses – 320 dead and 944 wounded – are regarded as one of the heaviest of the war on a single day.

At the end of November 1900, when the Boer capital cities had fallen in the first phase of the war, Kitchener took over from Roberts as commander of British forces. He tried to initiate peace talks with the Boers in February 1901, but the Boers' insistence on retaining their independence made the talks a failure.

Kitchener retaliated by enforcing Roberts's scorched-earth policy, destroying over 30 000 farms and several towns in the two republics. According to Sir George Arthur's *Life of Lord Kitchener*, he wrote the following in a letter: 'Owing to the vastness of the country the Boers can roam at pleasure, and being excessively mobile they are able to surprise any post not sufficiently on the alert. Every farm is to them an intelligence agency and a supply depot, so that it is almost impossible to surround or catch them … To meet some of the difficulties, I have determined to bring in the women from the more disturbed districts to laagers near the railway, and offer the burghers to join them there.'

Kitchener also began erecting thousands of blockhouses, each one linked to the next by barbed-wire barricades. He then launched large-scale raids to trap commandos between these fenced-off lines of blockhouses.

Kitchener enforced the concentration camp system, a stain on the

Lord Kitchener, First Earl of Khartoum and Broome. He departed for India by ship on 23 June 1902 to serve as commander of the British forces there, throwing his Anglo-Boer War archives into the Red Sea along the way.

British war effort in South Africa, with heavy-handed zeal. The system, which removed civilians to concentration camps, sought to break the guerrilla fighters' morale and prevent them from accessing supplies and information from the women who had stayed behind on the farms. Over 27 000 white and 24 000 black women and children died in the camps, under appalling conditions. The execution of this system was hugely controversial, not only in Europe but also in Britain.

On 31 May 1902, Kitchener and the Boer leaders signed the Peace of Vereeniging. At the stroke of a pen, the two republics lost their independence and became part of the British Empire. Kitchener went on to become commander in chief in India, and was appointed Secretary of State for War when the First World War broke out. In June 1916, he died at sea when the armoured cruiser HMS *Hampshire*, on which he was travelling to Russia, struck a mine and sank.

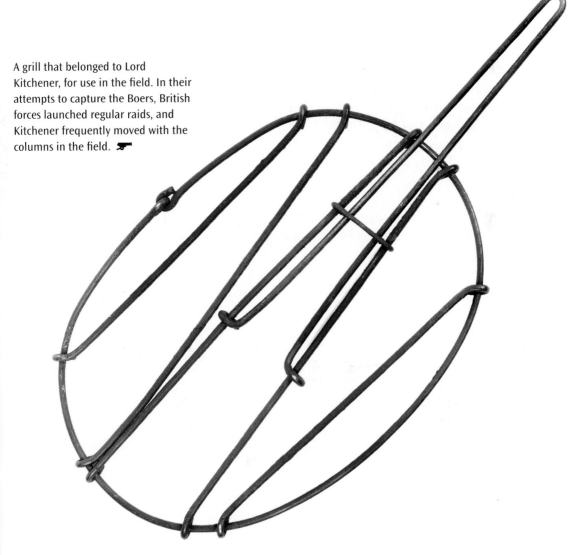

A grill that belonged to Lord Kitchener, for use in the field. In their attempts to capture the Boers, British forces launched regular raids, and Kitchener frequently moved with the columns in the field.

Lord Milner

Alfred Milner was appointed governor of the Cape Colony and high commissioner for southern Africa in 1897. He proved himself a capable official, serving, among others, as private secretary to the British minister of finance, director general of military finances in Egypt and chairman of the Board of Inland Revenue. He was also an outspoken imperialist.

On his arrival in South Africa, Milner quickly realised that Paul Kruger and the South African Republic represented a stumbling block for British imperialist aspirations. The political support that the republic enjoyed in the Cape Colony among members of the Afrikaner Bond, a political party, confirmed his suspicions that the South African Republic was Afrikaner nationalism's driving force.

When tension between the Transvaal and the British government neared breaking point, Milner saw military action as the solution. He engaged with Kruger at the Bloemfontein Conference, but had no real interest in a peaceful settlement. At his recommendation, therefore, the British government moved the goalposts in negotiations over issues such as Uitlander voting rights.

Lord Alfred Milner, first Viscount of St James's and Cape Town. He held the position of British high commissioner in southern Africa from 1897 to 1905.

The South African Republic's October 1899 ultimatum to the British government catalysed the war. Milner's political career came under intense scrutiny during the war; he had to report frequently to the British government about the prospects of a victory over the republics. In sharp contrast with Milner's prediction that the war would be over within three months, it lasted for almost three years.

Friction often arose between Milner and Kitchener, commander in chief of British forces in South Africa. It was Kitchener, in fact, who convinced Milner to make the concessions that led to the Peace of Vereeniging on 31 May 1902. On 24 May 1901, Milner was made a viscount as a reward for his contribution to the expansion of the empire.

After the war, Milner was nominated administrator and, later, governor of the two former republics, which were then being run as crown colonies. His objectives in this role were twofold: first, to strengthen British imperialism by entrenching British citizens in southern Africa; and, second, to rebuild the two new colonies with the help of a small group of hand-picked British officials, known as 'Milner's kindergarten'. Their common goal was to promote British interests.

Milner also implemented a policy of anglicising the civil service, much to the consternation of the Afrikaans-speaking population. He proceeded to make decisions that alienated him from the English-speaking South African population, too – such as importing cheap Chinese labour for the mines.

When the Conservative Party lost to Sir Henry Campbell-Bannerman's Liberal Party in the 1905 British general election, Milner was replaced and returned to Britain.

The seat on which Sir Alfred Milner sat during the Bloemfontein Conference, shortly before the outbreak of the war. In a letter to Lord Selborne before the conference, Milner wrote: 'My view has been and still is … that if we are perfectly determined we shall win without a fight or with a mere apology for one.'

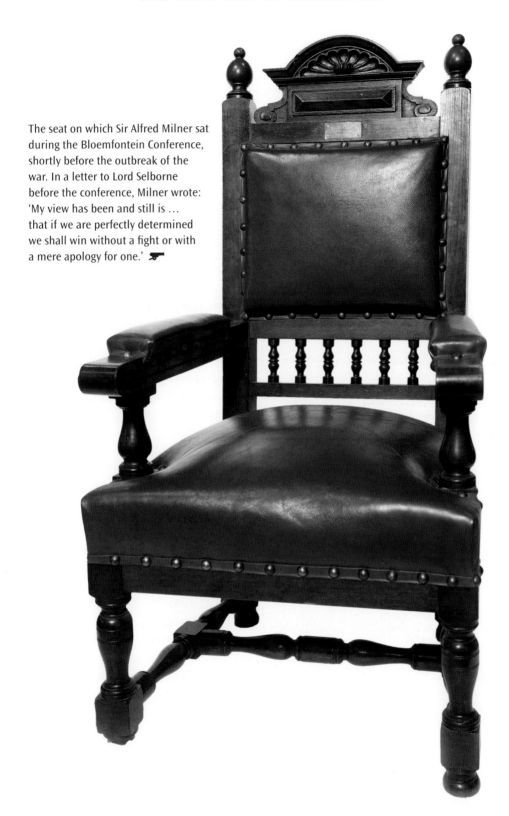

Winston Churchill

Winston Leonard Spencer-Churchill – future British prime minister and world leader – came into the world on 30 November 1874, in Blenheim Palace, the seat of the Dukes of Marlborough, in Oxfordshire. He was the son of Lord Randolph Churchill, a promising politician who passed away in 1895, aged only 44.

Winston Churchill on arrival in Durban after his escape from Pretoria. *Western Cape Archives*

Winston Churchill was accepted at the Royal Military College, Sandhurst, after several attempts at passing the entrance exam. Here, in February 1895, he was assigned to the 4th Queen's Own Hussars as second lieutenant. His military background led to his appointment as a journalist for the *Daily Graphic* to cover the Cuban War of Independence (1895–1898). He served in India in 1896, and participated in the Battle of Omdurman, in the Sudan, in 1898. As a part-time correspondent for the *Morning Post*, he gave a lively account of his experiences on campaign.

Churchill interrupted his military career in 1899, making himself available as a Conservative Party candidate in a parliamentary by-election in Oldham. He was not elected, however.

When the Anglo-Boer War broke out, Churchill left for South Africa as a *Morning Post* journalist. He would be neither the first Churchill to find himself in South Africa, nor the first journalist to emerge from his family. His aunt, Sarah Wilson (née Churchill), covered the siege of Mafeking as a *Daily Mail* journalist.

Churchill covered the battles at Ladysmith and surrounds. On arriving in Natal, he departed Estcourt for Ladysmith on 15 November 1899 aboard an armoured train with Captain Aylmer Haldane's men. At Chieveley station, however, a Boer commando attacked the train, which backtracked to about two miles outside the station, where it came under rifle and artillery fire, and partially derailed: the Boers had piled rocks on the line. Despite Churchill's valiant efforts to clear the rails and allow at least some of the soldiers to escape, he was captured, along with Haldane and 52 others. The prisoners of war were taken to Pretoria, where the officers were detained in the Staats Model School.

The Staats Model School, from which Churchill escaped. The photo shows British officers sitting on the stoep while guards patrol outside.

Churchill met Jan Smuts, the Transvaal attorney general, while in detention. The meeting sparked a friendship that would endure for more than four decades and two world wars. He considered it his duty to try to escape, taking his chance one night when the guards surrounding the school appeared distracted. He scaled the corrugated-iron fence that temporarily isolated the building and headed south through the darkened city, ending up at the railway line. He noticed a goods train at the station. As it passed him, he sprang onto it, hiding under a heap of sacks.

He jumped off the train near Witbank, continuing his journey on foot. He knocked on the door of a house that he hoped would belong to a British sympathiser. He was in luck: it was the house of John Howard, who supervised a nearby coal mine. Aided by Howard and others, Churchill stowed away on another goods train and crossed the border into Portuguese East Africa. The British consulate in Lourenço Marques (now Maputo) secured his passage by ship to reach Durban on 23 December 1899, where he received a hero's welcome.

Later in the war, his mother, Lady Churchill, would be instrumental in establishing the *Maine*, a hospital ship for wounded British soldiers.

The British press reported on Churchill's adventures in great detail, making him a household figure to the British public and furthering his political aspirations.

A Bible taken by a British soldier during the war. He gave it to Churchill years later, requesting Churchill to hand it over to Jan Smuts in the hope that it would find its way back to its original owner.

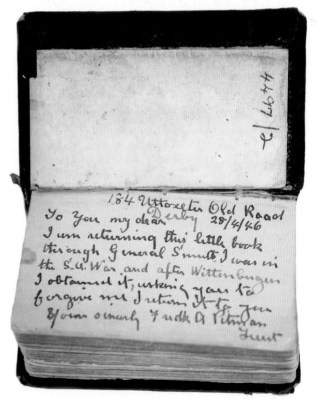

Emily Hobhouse

Emily Hobhouse, the studious daughter of an Anglican archdeacon, cared for her father for 15 years after the death of her mother. Through visits to her aunt and uncle, Lord and Lady Hobhouse, she was exposed to more liberal circles.

When her father passed away, she went to America, doing community work among the Cornish mineworkers in the small town of Virginia, Minnesota. She returned to England in 1898 and met Leonard H Courtney, a liberal Member of Parliament and campaigner for a peaceful settlement between Britain and the Boer republics.

In 1900, Hobhouse requested permission from the British government to represent the South African Women and Children Distress Fund on a visit to South Africa. She arrived in December of that year to dispense humanitarian help, in the form of food, clothing and other essentials, to the citizens of the two republics.

Britain's scorched-earth and concentration-camp policy disturbed Hobhouse deeply. Lord Kitchener gave her permission to visit the camps in the southern part of the Orange Free State, on condition that her work did not extend north of the Bloemfontein camps. The conditions in the concentration camps, which held primarily women and children, shocked and appalled her.

Her letters make it clear that she blamed the British government and the military authorities for the horrific conditions – shortages of suitable food, housing, clean water, clothing and sanitation – in the camps. She made her findings known in Britain on several occasions, and a number of liberal British newspapers published them.

Despite being labelled a traitor by her countrymen, Hobhouse arranged numerous public debates in Britain to inform the public about the state of affairs in the camps. She also compiled pamphlets and handouts, and distributed them publicly. This led to a public debate in Parliament. It was her information to which Sir Henry Campbell-Bannerman, the Liberal Party leader, referred when he made his well-known statement: 'When is a war not a war? When it is waged by methods of barbarism in South Africa.'

Thanks to Emily Hobhouse's protests, both friend and foe came to know the truth about the war in South Africa. She embarked on a second visit in October 1901, but martial law saw her returned to Britain before she could even set foot

Dutch artist Antoon van Welie painted this portrait of Emily Hobhouse.

on South African soil. Undeterred, she persisted in her protests and gatherings to inform the British public.

Her book about the war and its effects on civilian society, *The Brunt of The War and Where It Fell*, was published in 1902. After the Peace of Vereeniging in that same year, she was able to return to South Africa. She did so in 1903, and resolved to reconcile Boer and Brit. To help rebuild an impoverished people, she established several weaving and spinning schools, as well as a lace-making school in the town of Koppies.

Constrained by ill health, Hobhouse was unable to attend the unveiling, in December 1913, of the National Women's Monument in Bloemfontein, erected in honour of the women and children who had died in the concentration camps. She continued to serve in a humanitarian capacity, working with German orphans during the First World War. She died on 8 June 1926 and was laid to rest at the Women's Monument in Bloemfontein.

This pendant, set in platinum, is a token of appreciation for Emily Hobhouse's service to the women and children of the concentration camps. The farmers of the Orange Free State presented it to her in 1919. Its seven coloured diamonds hail from the Jagersfontein mine. Hobhouse bequeathed the pendant to Johanna Osborne, one of her pupils at the lace-making school in Koppies. Osborne's son donated it to the War Museum in 2011. 🔫

A tin of butterscotch sweets, which Emily Hobhouse gave to 16-year-old Johanna Roux of the farm Paardekraal, in the Wepener district. Johanna was incarcerated with her mother and other family members in the Bethulie concentration camp in the Orange Free State.

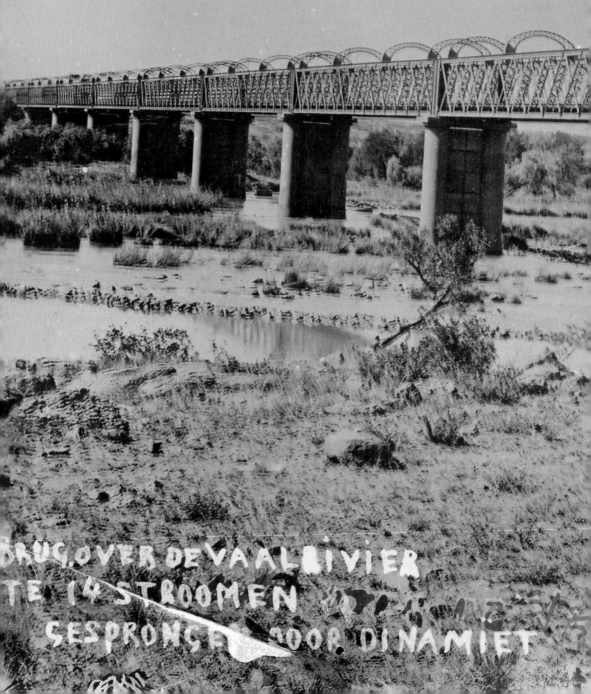

A railway bridge over the Vaal River, blown up with dynamite by the Boers. Republican forces tried to damage as much rail infrastructure as possible to prevent, or at least delay, the advance of British forces.

BRUG OVER DE VAALRIVIER TE 14 STROOMEN GESPRONGEN DOOR DINAMIET

Guerrilla Warfare and the Blockhouse System

Shortly before the fall of Bloemfontein, Boer forces decided to modify their strategy. President MT Steyn declared Kroonstad the new Orange Free State capital on 12 March 1900, and five days later held a war council meeting with President Paul Kruger, General Piet Joubert and 22 senior officers.

The council made several decisions about how the war would be continued, the most important being to take the offensive and divide the commandos into smaller, more mobile units. In General Christiaan de Wet's words: 'We need to attack the enemy continually, quickly and unexpectedly.' Joubert believed that, in this way, they could exact the greatest possible enemy losses while suffering the fewest losses of their own. Another important decision was to do away with the unwieldy wagon encampments, comprising many women and children, that often accompanied the commandos, slowing them down.

The war council also recognised the importance of communication systems to the British war effort, and resolved to destroy railway lines, tunnels, bridges and telegraph lines.

Demolishing the bridges over the Tugela, Orange, Vet and Vaal rivers required specialist knowledge, however, so this kind of work was initially carried out by trained employees of the Nederlandsch-Zuid-Afrikaansche Spoorweg-maatschappij (NZASM). As the war progressed, however, this kind of work fell increasingly to selected groups of burghers. In addition, British supply columns were attacked and small garrisons besieged.

As a countermeasure, British forces began, in December 1900, to erect fortifications and barbed-wire barricades to protect railway lines, supply routes and other strategically important points. These forts soon became known as 'blockhouses', after the block-shaped structure of the first multi-level forts.

The blockhouses were built of concrete, sandstone or any suitable local materials. The blockhouse at Prieska, in the Cape Colony, for example, included tiger's-eye quartz in its construction. The Royal Engineers were tasked with erecting these structures, and the first blockhouses were sited near bridges and smaller level crossings.

Of course, this turn of events increased both the cost of the war and the demand for soldiers to man the new blockhouses. The blockhouses had

Captain Henri Slegtkamp, a Dutchman by birth, was notorious among the British for his skill in destroying rail infrastructure. He used, among other tactics, a 'train wrecker' to derail trains. He served in Captain Danie Theron's Reconnaissance Corps before leading a corps of 50 proficient rail saboteurs.

An example of a 'train wrecker', used by the Boers to derail trains. They would place dynamite and part of a Martini-Henry rifle bolt containing a round under the rail. When a train passed, its weight depressed the trigger, firing the round and detonating the dynamite.

'The Boer Forces were organised into commandos, each of some five hundred mounted riflemen, their mobile tactics of hit-and-run well suited to operations across the local terrain of which they had intimate knowledge. Their effectiveness would so impress Winston Churchill that more than forty years later, as Prime Minister during the Second World War, he would order the formation of commandos for raiding purposes.'
– Celia Sandys, *Churchill, Wanted Dead or Alive*

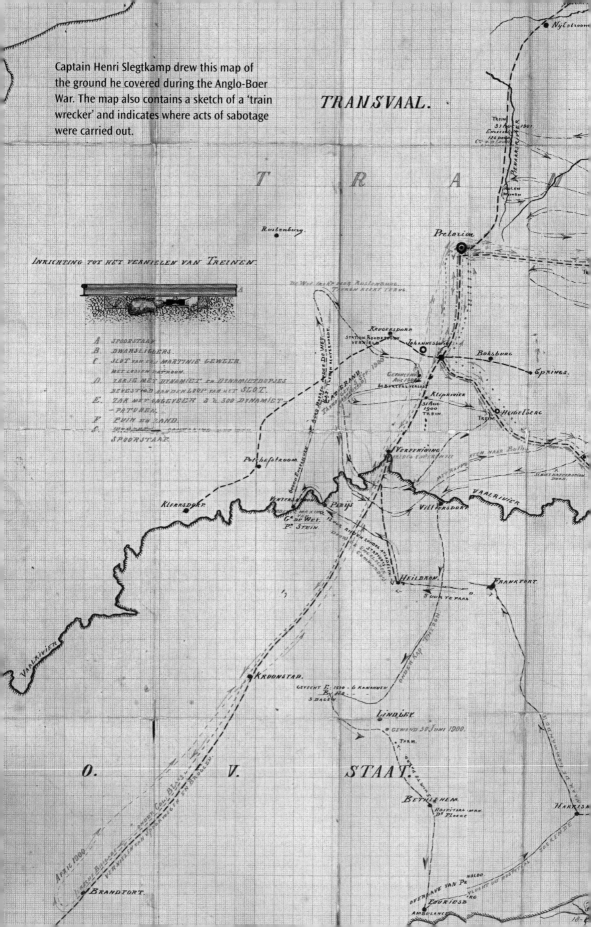

Captain Henri Slegtkamp drew this map of
the ground he covered during the Anglo-Boer
War. The map also contains a sketch of a 'train
wrecker' and indicates where acts of sabotage
were carried out.

TRANSVAAL.

Nylstroom

Rustenburg

Pretoria

INRICHTING TOT HET VERNIELEN VAN TREINEN.

Krugersdorp
STATION ROODEBOOM
VERNIEL
Johannesburg
Boksburg
Springs

Kliprivier
Heidelberg

A. SPOORSTAAF.
B. DWARSLIGGERS.
C. SLOT VAN EEN MARTINIE GEWEER.
   MET LOSSEN PATROON.
D. ZAKJE MET DYNAMIET EN DYNAMIETDOPJES
   BEVESTIGD AAN DEN LOOP VAN HET SLOT.
E. ZAK MET ONGEVEER 2 à 300 DYNAMIET
   -PATRONEN.
F. PUIN EN ZAND.
G. SPOORSTAAF.

Potchefstroom

Vereeniging

Vaalrivier

Klerksdorp
Parijs
Villiersdorp

Heilbron
Frankfort

Kroonstad

Lindley

O.   V.   STAAT.

Bethlehem

Brandtfort

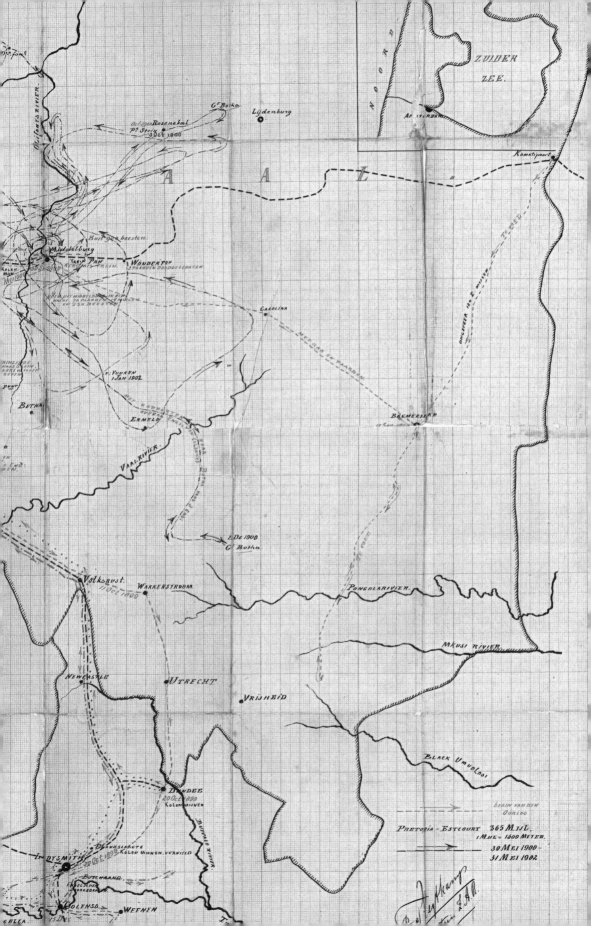

ZUIDER
ZEE.

NOORD

AMSTERDAM

KOMATIPOORT

Oliphantsrivier.

Dr. Fort

Gl Botha
Oct 1900 Rosenekal
Pr Steis 31 Oct 1900

Lijdenburg

T U G E L A

ZAAL

Buit ons beesten.

Middelburg

Tafel Pan   WONDERFON
2 Fanden Doodgeschoten

Carolina

Nieuw de Paarden

Onseelta na E Miljo

Bremerslep
15 Sept 190

Ermelo

v. Vuuren
1 Jan 1902

Bethml

Vaalrivier.

2 De 1900
Gl Botha

Volksrust.
11 Oct 1900

Wakkerstroom.

Pongolarivier.

Mkusi Rivier.

Newcastle

Utrecht

Vrijheid

Dundee
20 Oct 1899
Kolenmijnen

Black Umvolosi

Buffelo Rivier

begin van den
Oorlog

Glandslagte
Kolen Mijnen vernield

Pretoria - Estcourt   365 Mijl.
1 Mijl = 1600 Meter.

Ladysmith
30 Oct 1899

Boschrand.

Engelschen
voorgekomen

Colenso   Weenen

30 Mei 1900 -
31 Mei 1902

great strategic value, nonetheless, and the system was extended at the beginning of 1901. British military authorities began dividing the republics into 'camps' by erecting lines of blockhouses in a grid pattern. They intended to use large-scale raids to drive the commandos into these blockhouse lines; creating these 'traps' was part of Kitchener's strategy.

To make the blockhouses cheaper and less time-consuming to erect, Major Spring Robert Rice of the Royal Engineers designed the corrugated-iron Rice blockhouse. These structures, costing a mere £16 per unit to erect, were manufactured in Pretoria, Bloemfontein and Middelburg. A detachment of about seven soldiers, under a non-commissioned officer, manned each Rice blockhouse.

Blockhouse guard life was tedious. To while away the time and relieve the monotony, soldiers kept wild animals such as baboons, lizards and meerkats as pets and often carved their names, and the names of their regiments, into surrounding rocks.

The blockhouse system may have made Boer movements more difficult, but it did not deliver results commensurate with the resources and time invested in it. The commandos pressed on with their guerrilla campaign.

The blockhouses that still stand in many parts of South Africa today are among the few palpable reminders of a war waged over a century ago.

Pliers used by burgher MC Howell van Petrus Steyn to cut the wire barricades strung between blockhouses. The pliers were part of the British military inventory, as they bear a British mark, called the 'hoenderspoor' (chicken spoor) by the Boers. The British later used steel cabling, which was harder to cut. The commandos would sometimes chase herds of cattle through the barricades to damage them enough for the burghers to make their way through.

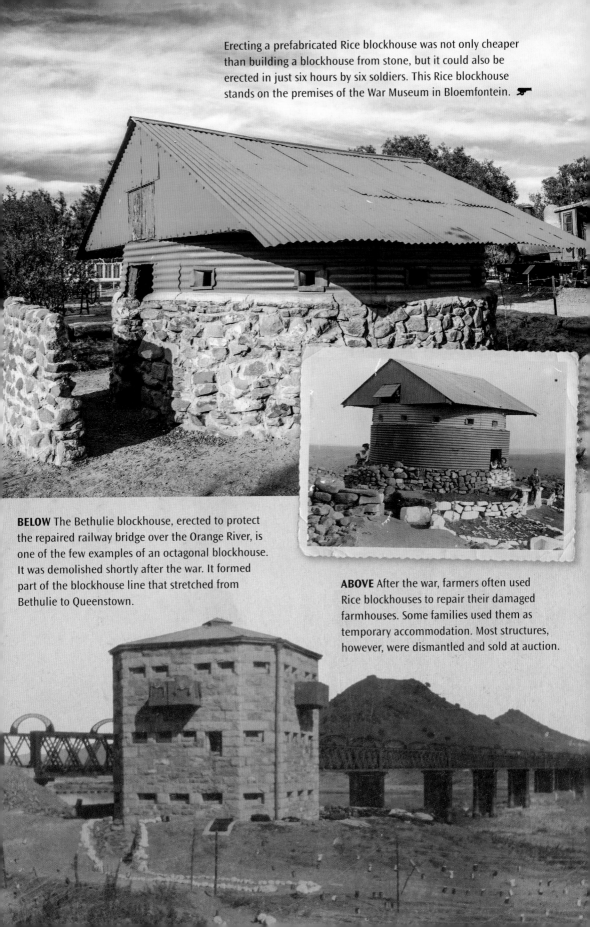

Erecting a prefabricated Rice blockhouse was not only cheaper than building a blockhouse from stone, but it could also be erected in just six hours by six soldiers. This Rice blockhouse stands on the premises of the War Museum in Bloemfontein.

BELOW The Bethulie blockhouse, erected to protect the repaired railway bridge over the Orange River, is one of the few examples of an octagonal blockhouse. It was demolished shortly after the war. It formed part of the blockhouse line that stretched from Bethulie to Queenstown.

ABOVE After the war, farmers often used Rice blockhouses to repair their damaged farmhouses. Some families used them as temporary accommodation. Most structures, however, were dismantled and sold at auction.

Sannaspos, 31 March 1900

After the fall of Bloemfontein, on 13 March 1900, Lord Roberts ordered Captain Charles Amphlett's small force of 300 men to stand sentry over the waterworks at Sannaspos, east of Bloemfontein. Knowing how important water was for Lord Roberts's impressive force in Bloemfontein, General Christiaan de Wet targeted the waterworks in what would become the war's first guerrilla attack.

De Wet launched his plan on 28 March. He sent his 1 500-strong force and its nine artillery pieces on a detour to the waterworks. What he did not know, however, was that Brigadier General George

A knapsack that Commandant Sarel Haasbroek took from a British officer at Sannaspos. Haasbroek's son used the knapsack until after the war.

Broadwood had received a simultaneous report that a large republican force was on the move east of Bloemfontein.

Broadwood's force of 1 700 men and two Royal Horse Artillery batteries were in the Thaba Nchu area of the Free State at the time (Sannaspos is almost halfway between Thaba Nchu and Bloemfontein). Unbeknown to De Wet, Broadwood decided to fall back to Bloemfontein via Sannaspos.

De Wet divided his force so that he could cut Amphlett's force off if Amphlett tried to fall back to Thaba Nchu. He left most of his men, and his artillery, to take up positions in the low hills northeast of the waterworks. With the rest of his men – about 500 in number – he dug in along the high banks at Koornspruitdrif, west of Sannaspos. His plan was to launch artillery fire on the British garrison at the waterworks from the northeast. The British would then flee westward to Bloemfontein – straight into his ambush at Koornspruit.

On the morning of 31 March, De Wet received word that a large British force was approaching, but chose to proceed with his plans. Needing the British to flee his attack in a specific direction, he ordered a few rounds of grapeshot to be fired at Broadwood's force. As De Wet had foreseen, this bewildered the British; in the ensuing chaos, they fled towards Bloemfontein, into the path of De Wet's ambush.

The retreating British vanguard, comprising a long convoy of wagons, vanished from the main force's view, allowing De Wet's forces to capture it without the rear guard suspecting a thing. At the very last minute, a British officer, sensing that something was amiss, raised the alarm.

The battle that followed saw the British suffer heavy losses. Broadwood managed to make it through Koornspruit with a part of his force, however, and to meet reinforcements from Bloemfontein at Boesmans Kop, but not before losing seven guns, ammunition, his convoy of over 105 wagons and many draught animals. In addition, the Boers took almost 430 prisoners of war, wounded 134 and killed 18.

In the end, De Wet did not manage to sabotage the waterworks.

Rieck & Co.   WINSBURG, O.R.C.

Commandant Sarel Haasbroek.

A bandolier that belonged to 24-year-old burgher Gerhardus Hubertus Goosen of Senekal, who perished at Sannaspos on 31 March 1900.

Roodewal, 7 June 1900

With the fall of the republican capitals, Lord Roberts and the British government were confident that Boer leaders would approach them soon with conditions for peace. At this stage, the British army's critically important communication systems stretched over a very long distance, straight through hostile territory.

The Boers had destroyed the rail bridge over the Rhenoster River after the fall of Kroonstad. This had caused a significant quantity of provisions to accumulate at Rooiwal (or Roodewal), a small station between Kroonstad and the Vaal River. The station was guarded by troops of the 4th (Nottinghamshire) Volunteer Battalion of the Derbyshire Regiment and the Railway Pioneer Corps under Captain AGW Grant.

After trying to convince Grant to surrender, General Christiaan de Wet attacked the train station with a force of 80 men and one artillery piece on 7 June. The British resisted –

from behind improvised ramparts made from mailbags and bales of blankets – for a full five hours.

Fearing that the Boers would detonate the station's ammunition stockpile, which included lyddite rounds, the British had no choice but to surrender. Eight men were killed, and 24 wounded. The Boers seized clothing, ammunition, champagne, food supplies and over 2 500 mailbags laden with gifts for British soldiers, such as tinned plum puddings.

De Wet also plundered several ammunition caches. He hid them on his farm Rooipoort, which was nearby, in a stockpile that would prove useful in the war's later stages. The republican force then destroyed the rest of the materiel, valued at £100 000, in a spectacular firework display.

The Roodewal incident compelled the British government to assure the British taxpayer that the war would be brought to a speedy end. Shortly after his arrival in Pretoria, Lord Roberts was informed about the Roodewal attack and ordered De Wet's home on Rooipoort farm, in the Orange Free State, to be razed.

General Christiaan de Wet in 1912 with some of the items, including a bas-relief (see opposite page), given to him as mementos during a visit to Europe after the war.

'While the Boers were busy [opening the mailbags] one of the
prisoners of war [a British soldier] came to me and asked whether
they could also open some of the mailbags and take some of
the parcels. Take them, I said – whichever ones, and however
many, you want. Everything had to burned in any event …
It was peculiar to see two hundred troops plundering their
own mail. Eventually, they became so selective that even
the plum puddings no longer counted as treats.'
– Christiaan de Wet, describing a Roodewal scene, in *Die Stryd tussen Boer en Brit*

Since before 1899, St Petersburg in Russia had been home to a large Swiss
community. Their admiration for De Wet's victory at Roodewal inspired them to
have this bas-relief made, set in a wooden frame of Russian birch. It was sent
with the following message: 'To the brave General de Wet, hardened defender of
oppressed freedom. In memory of our strong conviction in the Boers' victory.'

Brandwater Basin, 15 July–9 August 1900

It took some weeks for Lord Roberts's forces to recover fully from the dysentery epidemic that had swept through the British camp after the fall of Bloemfontein. His advance to Pretoria, with about 44 000 soldiers, commenced on 3 May 1900. When Kroonstad fell, on 12 May, Orange Free State forces retreated eastwards to the Bethlehem region. They tried to take up positions there, but the British forced them further back.

The Orange Free State force came together in the Brandwater Basin, near Fouriesburg, in the eastern part of the republic, where 4 400 burghers would eventually lay down their weapons in one of the Boers' biggest setbacks of the guerrilla phase.

The Free State war council, fearing that Lieutenant General Archibald Hunter's 18 000-strong contingent would surround the Boer gathering, chose to divide the men into three groups. The primary force – General Christiaan de Wet's 2 000 men, with President MT Steyn and the government camp in its care – deflected to the Kroonstad/Heilbron region on 15 July. Shortly before De Wet departed, General Paul Roux, a minister, was appointed assistant commander in chief and new commander of the second force, comprising about eight commandos. General Jan Crowther led the third force.

Roux ordered both remaining forces to depart the following day, 16 July. His force was to retire to Bloemfontein, and Crowther's to Bethlehem. A small commando under former commander in chief Marthinus Prinsloo would stay behind to keep watch until all the commandos had departed.

Roux waited for another two commandos to join him, contravening war council orders. His delay gave the gathering British forces time to surround him, occupying strategic points along the mountain passes around the Brandwater Basin and Golden Gate.

To make matters worse, Prinsloo began questioning Roux's appointment. Having resigned his post the previous month due to illness, his claims that he, and not Roux, was the leader of the remaining forces unsettled the burghers and officers, and wasted valuable time.

So it was that the Boers forfeited their chance to escape. By the end of July, Roux and his men were surrounded. The leadership question was put to a vote; panicked officers chose Prinsloo.

To prevent their ammunition from falling into British hands, the Boers at Brandwater Basin destroyed their ammunition supplies before surrendering. This is what some of their melted ammunition looked like. The heat involved was so intense that, to this day, grass will not grow in certain spots in the area. Youngsters in Prinsloo's camp told, years later, of the documents they were ordered to burn in the days before the capitulation – documents that likely comprised the Orange Free State military archive. 🔫

Meanwhile, Prinsloo had sent Stephanus Vilonel, a former commandant from Winburg who had laid down his weapon in June 1900, to Hunter to petition for a ceasefire (Vilonel was in detention after a Boer war council had sentenced him to five years' imprisonment, so Prinsloo used him as a messenger). Hunter demanded unconditional surrender, to which Prinsloo agreed.

Half the Free State force – Prinsloo, Roux and nine commandos numbering almost 4 400 men – laid down their weapons between 30 July and 9 August. The British later released Prinsloo on parole, but sent Roux and his men to a prisoner-of-war camp in Ceylon (now Sri Lanka).

The controversy surrounding the events at Brandwater Basin exiled Prinsloo from Afrikaner ranks after the war. The suspicion that he had committed treason was deepened when he and his 4 400 men received additional repatriation assistance after the war.

At the start of the war, Orange Free State forces under General Marthinus Prinsloo (circled) invaded Natal. Prinsloo was later elected commander in chief. After surrendering in the Brandwater Basin, he was sent to Simon's Town as a prisoner of war, which is where this photo of him with British officers was taken.

British troops in the Brandwater Basin at the time of Prinsloo's surrender.

Bergendal, August 1900

Shortly before British forces occupied Pretoria, President Paul Kruger and the South African Republic government retreated to Machadodorp. It did not take long for General Redvers Buller's Natal Field Force, which had invaded the Transvaal from Natal, to start its advance on Machadodorp.

A helmet insignia of the Transvaal police force, or Zuid-Afrikaansche Republiek Politie (Zarp). The eagle echoes that in the Transvaal coat of arms. ☞

The 11 000-strong advancing force occupied the towns of Volksrust, Standerton and Ermelo along the way. Other units under Generals John French and Ian Hamilton joined Buller in an attempt to surround the Transvaal government and commandos. The combined force of nearly 20 000 men was widely spread.

General Louis Botha established a relatively long line of defence – nearly 80 km – to defend the railway line, the Transvaal government's line of communication with the outside world. In preparation for the assault on their final positions in the eastern Transvaal, the Boers mustered several pieces of artillery – including the four Long Toms. It would be the first and last time that all four of these guns would be deployed in a single campaign.

The Battle of Bergendal began on 21 August 1900. It lasted for a few days, and constituted a series of skirmishes between British forces and various Boer commandos, all along the railway line that ran east from the town of Belfast. Since Botha was headquartered at Dalmanutha station, this engagment is sometimes referred to as the Battle of Dalmanutha.

Buller's troops had to cross the farm Bergendal, but about 70 men of the Transvaal police (Zuid-Afrikaansche Republiek Politie, or Zarp), had taken up positions there. The battle climaxed on 27 August in a three-hour British bombardment of the hills where the Zarp force had dug in. The heavy shelling issued from both naval and field guns.

The British followed up their bombardment with frontal and flank assaults by the 1st Devonshires, the Rifle Brigade, the Gordon Highlanders and the Royal Inniskilling Fusiliers. Zarp forces were short of ammunition, and consequently had to

A Boer Mauser with a shortened muzzle.
The Transvaal coat of arms, and the
inscription 'Boer War 1899, 1900, 1901'
appears on one side of the stock.

fire very selectively. The enemy crept ever closer to their positions, which they eventually had to relinquish. The intense resistance that they had put up, with only rifles and a 37-mm Maxim-Nordenfelt quick-firing pom-pom at their disposal, inspired other commandos to hold their positions, however. Their courage also earned them the admiration of senior British officers, including Lord Roberts.

The road to Machadodorp was clear after the Battle of Bergendal. A joint sitting of the Transvaal and Orange Free State governments decided to send President Kruger to Europe, where he would campaign for support of the republican war effort.

Members of the Zuid-Afrikaansche Republiek Politie (Zarp) at Fort Hendrina in Louis Trichardt, in the northern Transvaal, shortly before the start of the war. Members of the republican police distinguished themselves during the Battle of Bergendal with a valiant defence of their position.

The State Mint in the Field

When the Kruger government and its senior officials retreated to Machadodorp after the occupation of Pretoria, they took with them the South African Republic archives and the republic's currency and gold reserves. The gold had an estimated value of £750 000.

In Machadodorp, the treasurer and auditor general met the republic's financial and administrative obligations from two goods carriages. Accurate records were kept of all payments through *gouvernementsnote* (government notes), which were backed by the gold reserves. The state mint issued the first of these *gouvernementsnote* in great haste shortly before the government left Pretoria. It is dated 28 May 1900 and embossed with the great seal of the South African Republic.

After the Battle of Bergendal in August 1900, the government moved to Nelspruit, in the far eastern Transvaal. By the end of 1900, the state coffers were almost empty. The decision was made to remedy the shortfall by issuing a second set of *gouvernementsnote* using the printing press of the *Zoutpansberg Wachter*, a newspaper in Pietersburg. The quality of this set – valued at £220 000 and dated 1 February 1901, 1 March 1901 and 1 April 1901 – was poor. When General HCO Plummer occupied Pietersburg, British troops destroyed the entire printing press.

The third and final set of *gouvernementsnote* was issued in 1902. Called the Pilgrim's Rest set, it was printed under supervision of burgher PJ Klopper of the Staatsdrukkerij te Velde (State Mint in the Field) and dated 1 March 1902, 1 April 1902 and 1 May 1902. The poor quality of the paper used means that few of these have survived intact.

Like the Mafeking Siege notes, the *gouvernementsnote* surely speak to the extraordinary perseverance and ingenuity of officials on both sides during the war.

The building and printing equipment of the *Zoutpansberg Wachter*, destroyed by General HCO Plummer's forces after the fall of Pietersburg – though not before British officers had used the press to print a newspaper in English.

Veldponde (Field Pounds)

The South African Republic government may have decamped to the eastern Transvaal, but it still had to meet its financial obligations in order to continue to finance the war. Officials also felt that for as long as the Transvaal government could continue to issue currency, the population would believe that it, and not the British forces that had occupied Pretoria, was the republic's legitimate government.

To do this, it was decided to turn the gold from the Pretoria Mint into coins. Thanks to General Ben Viljoen, the government came by additional gold reserves from the Pilgrim's Rest mines. A Mint Commission would oversee the minting of the coins.

The Staatsdrukkerij te Velde (State Mint in the Field), established under supervision of a teacher, PJ Klopper, used equipment belonging to the Transvaal Gold Mining Estates company at Pilgrim's Rest, and ensured that Klopper was supported in his role by skilled artisans. An Irishman, Michael Cooney, helped to refine and purify the gold; Scottish ironsmith William Reid created the stamps for pressing the coins; and another Irishman, Dick Graham, was charged with melting the gold.

PJ Klopper (circled) with other members of the State Mint in the Field.

The first six stamps designed by Klopper cracked, and it was only on the seventh attempt that they succeeded. The stamps were used to press the coins by means of a small hand press, at a time when forging coins was the norm.

To make the coins, planchets were first pressed from strips of gold. The strips needed to be of a specific thickness, which the Transvaal Gold Mining Estates' rollers helped to ensure. The gold had to be heated and cooled several times, a process in which Graham was skilled. Some of the coins that were made using gold from the surrounding diggings developed fine cracks, which Klopper remedied by adding mercury from the Transvaal Gold Mining Estates' first-aid supplies.

Sources differ about the exact number of *veldponde*, or field pounds, that were minted, but it is thought that 986 were made. As a token of gratitude to the members of the State Mint in the Field, the South African Republic government awarded each man a special medal, on which a *veldpond* was mounted.

A brooch made from a *veldpond* framed by four rifles. The inscription reads 'JP Anna, 1900'. *Veldponde* quickly became highly prized souvenirs; scores were later made into jewellery.

A rare one-pound *gouvernementsnoot*, printed on 1 May 1902 at Pilgrim's Rest. The paper on which the last two series of notes were printed was repurposed from sources such as school exercise books and the ledgers of the Transvaal Gold Mining Estates company. The notes were also known as 'goedvoors' ('good fors'). The Pilgrim's Rest notes were signed by AP Brugman, acting auditor general, and Paul de Villiers, acting treasurer general of the South African Republic. ✐

A *veldpond* with the monogram 'ZAR 1902' on one side and 'Een Pond' (one pound) on the other. The coins were designed by PJ Klopper. ✐

Attorney General Jan Smuts was tasked with removing the Transvaal's mint and gold reserves from Pretoria shortly before the town's occupation. This involved threatening a stubborn National Bank official with a revolver to convince him to hand over the State Mint's gold reserves (the bank managed the State Mint). Unminted coins, or 'kaalponde' ('bare pounds'), such as the one on the left, formed part of the reserves. The South African Republic government later put these into circulation, as many people, especially among black communities in the northern and eastern Transvaal, had little confidence in the *gouvernementsnote*.

Ysterspruit, 25 February 1902

By February 1902, all commandos in the republics were feeling, keenly, an acute shortage of supplies of every kind, as well as materiel and horses. Plundering British forces was one of the methods they used to restock.

After Colonel SB von Donop occupied Wolmaransstad, in the western Transvaal, on 8 February, the British garrison there had to be provisioned. General Koos de la Rey, leader of the western Transvaal forces, had received intelligence from his scouts that a substantial convoy was planning to supply the garrison. He started planning a strategy to attack the convoy, knowing full well that it would have an escort.

Before long, De la Rey's scouts brought news that a 156-wagon convoy had left Wolmaransstad to provision in Klerksdorp. The convoy, under Lieutenant Colonel WC Anderson, had a 700-strong escort from the 5th Imperial Yeomanry, the 1st Northumberland Fusiliers, and mounted infantry from Paget's Horse. The last-mentioned unit had two guns and a pom-pom in tow.

De la Rey's strategy involved commandos under Generals Johannes Cilliers, Petrus Liebenberg and Jan Kemp attacking the convoy from three directions. The slow-moving convoy had struck camp at Ysterspruit for one last time, before embarking on the final leg of their journey to Klerksdorp. De la Rey knew that a surprise attack would improve his chances of success.

By midnight on a rainy, misty 24 February, all three commandos were in position. Some British guards ran into Kemp's camp, however, and a brief skirmish erupted. Anderson issued orders for an early departure. At 4.30 am, the convoy moved off, with soldiers posted in the vanguard, rear guard and flanks.

Liebenberg led the Boer attack on the vanguard. The three commandos did not attack simultaneously, however, so Liebenberg was beaten back.

Cilliers' force was ready for the third attack: it stormed the convoy with a vengeance, under heavy rifle fire, breaching Anderson's defences and sowing panic. The convoy splintered.

Liebenberg seized the guns, firing on the fleeing convoy with its own artillery, which sowed even deeper panic. Scores of wagons rolled over; others foundered in the Ysterspruit mud.

So it was that De la Rey plundered 156 wagons, 150 horses, 1 500 mules, and all the guns and pom-poms, not to mention half a million rounds of ammunition. He did, however, make two wagons available to the Royal Army Medical Corps to transport the British wounded to Klerksdorp.

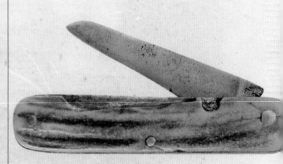

A pocket knife that burgher Jurie Johannes Human took from a British officer, Lieutenant RT Jones.

This telescope belonged to Jurie Johannes Human, who perished in the Battle of Ysterspruit. Human also took this from Lieutenant Jones, whom he had fatally wounded in the Groot Marico.

These British soldiers are using the same pattern of telescope as shown above. They are tending a pom-pom gun.

Hensoppers and Joiners

The fall of Bloemfontein (on 13 March 1900) and Pretoria (on 5 June 1900) demoralised many republican fighters. On 15 March 1900, Lord Roberts issued a proclamation promising that burghers who laid down their weapons would earn passes to return to their farms and homes.

Scores, consequently, took the Oath of Neutrality, with some believing that further conflict was futile, and others withdrawing due to material considerations. Later, the suffering of women and children in the concentration camps would compel many burghers to end their fight. These became known as 'hensoppers' ('hands-uppers').

By the end of 1900, some of these hensoppers had joined British-sanctioned Burgher Peace Committees, dispatched to try to convince Boer fighters to withdraw from combat. The British quickly realised that some of these burghers were prepared to switch sides; in 1901, the National Scouts came into being in the Transvaal.

The 'joiners', as the National Scouts became known to the Boers, were seen as traitors. Some joiners who fell captive to Boer commandos were tried and, sometimes, executed. This engendered a bitterness that was to endure beyond the end of the war, with joiners being shunned by society in the former republics.

Joiners from Winburg who served under Captain Oloff Bergh (circled). For years afterwards, the Winburg community remained divided over the issue of the joiners, a division felt even in the church; it spilled over into a rift in the Winburg congregation.

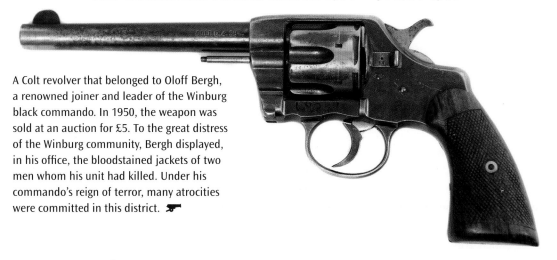

A Colt revolver that belonged to Oloff Bergh, a renowned joiner and leader of the Winburg black commando. In 1950, the weapon was sold at an auction for £5. To the great distress of the Winburg community, Bergh displayed, in his office, the bloodstained jackets of two men whom his unit had killed. Under his commando's reign of terror, many atrocities were committed in this district. 🔫

By February 1901, a 60-strong National Scouts corps was lodged in a camp near Pretoria. From here, the unit launched reconnaissance excursions, gathering intelligence about Boer commando positions and supplying it to the British. Taking an oath of allegiance to the Crown was mandatory for each member.

From October of that year onwards, former Boer officers such as General Andries Petrus Johannes Cronjé (the brother of general Piet Cronjé) launched large-scale National Scouts recruitment drives in the Transvaal concentration camps, among other locations. Only volunteers and bona fide Transvaal burghers were accepted into National Scouts ranks.

By the end of the war, the National Scouts had nine divisions, each with its own officer, under the overall command of Major EHM Leggett.

The Orange River Colony Volunteers (ORC Volunteers) were the Free State equivalent of the National Scouts. They came into being late in the war, however, with two divisions forming in March 1902. One division, containing 200 men, was stationed under former commandant Stephanus Gerhardus Vilonel in Winburg; former commandant Piet de Wet (brother of General Christiaan de Wet) led the other, containing 248 men, from its Heilbron base.

Captain PHJ Blakemore led the ORC Volunteers, whose short-lived existence involved reconnaissance excursions, night attacks and British column support. According to the British review of April 1902, this unit comprised 358 men; at the end of the war, it had 448 members.

From January 1901, the South African Constabulary's Colonel Charles Ridley also took joiners into service. Initially known as the Burgher Police, they later became the Farmers' Guard.

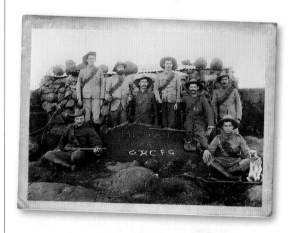

The capitulators that the South African Constabulary took into service. The Burgher Police, later known as the Farmers' Guard, comprised Orange Free State burghers who actively supported the British war effort against their compatriots.

The Black Commando of Winburg

During the course of the war, Lord Kitchener realised that he was going to need the help of black South Africans, due to their familiarity with the districts in which the commandos were active. The British government's initial decision was not to involve black people in the war, but its military broke with this resolution to recruit an ever-increasing number.

It fell to black recruits, initially, to guard strategic installations such as bridges, but from 1901 they were armed and deployed in offensive roles. Promises of land, political rights and payment drew increasing numbers into the war on Britain's side.

By 1901, the Boer commandos in the Orange Free State – specifically, the Winburg area – had encountered a unit comprising 400 to 500 armed black men under white officers. The unit was notorious: not only did they attack commandos but they also destroyed farms and abused Boer women and children. Worse, the unit's officers – including Captain Oloff Bergh – were Free State joiners.

In one incident, the Winburg black commando murdered three burghers from Commandant Sarel Haasbroek's commando in particularly brutal fashion at Doornberg, about 32 km from Senekal. In retaliation, Haasbroek's commando captured and executed 18 members of Bergh's commando.

Two armed black men who were recruited for the British forces.

The Winburg black commando under Captain Oloff Bergh (circled).

A British soldier removes a hidden note from the collar of a black spy who worked for the British forces.

A hat that belonged to 21-year-old Willem (William) Edward Scott of Vaalkrans farm in the Winburg district. Scott was captured and fatally shot on 26 May 1901 by the Winburg black commando. The words 'Gestorben door verraad' ('Dead through treason') appear on his tombstone. 🔫

Commando Rations

by Dané Swanepoel

In the Anglo-Boer War years, the ordinary citizen was obliged to go on commando with his horse, a firearm and enough rations for about eight days. The republican governments undertook to provide for the commandos thereafter. They were unprepared, unfortunately, for the numbers of men for whom they would need to provide rations.

In the early stages of the war, tins of beef, mutton, ham, salmon and even sardines were ferried to the Boers at the front. After a few months, however, it fell to the men's families to feed them, or else they would commandeer rations. Meals were largely prepared by the grooms, who would also see to coffee.

Meat was a popular component of victuals and was, for the most part, relatively freely available. At the beginning of the war, beef and mutton were fairly common. In the later phases of the war, however, thousands of cattle were slaughtered as part of Britain's scorched-earth policy, so the commandos took to shooting game. Biltong and dried sausage, which kept for long periods, were in high demand. Donkey and horse meat were consumed reluctantly in desperate times.

Poultry such as chicken, duck, goose and turkey thinned out quickly; game birds such as guinea fowl, spur fowl and pigeon were regarded as delicacies. Within months, eggs also became a luxury. The Boers supplemented their diets by catching freshwater fish and even terrapins.

Initially, starch such as bread and army biscuits were supplied readily. A favourite, however, was the fresher and far tastier *stormjaers* and *maagbommen*. A *stormjaer* was a type of vetkoek – unsweetened dough deep-fried in oil – while *maagbommen* loosely resembled pancakes and were cooked on hot rocks next to the cooking fire. Macaroni and rice were also available.

Putu-pap, a kind of maize porridge, quickly replaced bread on commando. At times, it was the commando members' only meal. The men ate the

The army biscuit, or 'dog biscuit', part of British soldiers' rations during the war. The names of four British soldiers – B Collins, GH Smith, JR Ross and JE Wright – appear on the back of this biscuit. To eat the biscuits, which were very hard and unpalatable, the soldiers usually broke them with their rifle stocks or bayonets before soaking them in water or tea. They sometimes even painted scenes onto the biscuits.

porridge with fat or sauce, and sometimes added biltong, bacon or offal for a little flavour and colour.

Coffee, the Boers' national beverage, became increasingly scarce as the war progressed. To make their *Boeretroos* (Boer's comfort or consolation) last longer, commando members and women in the field mixed real coffee with adulterations such as corn, peas, burnt peach or apricot stones and even sweet potato. The most popular coffee substitute was the root of the shepherd's tree, or *witgatboom*, dried, finely chopped, roasted and ground.

Fresh produce was scarce; dried fruit, raisins, tinned fruit, and longer-lasting produce such as potatoes, onions and quinces were far more common on commando.

It was easier, in fact, for the commandos to access fresh fruit during the guerrilla phase; the commandos were more mobile, and could make stops at farms that still had orchards. In the bushveld, commandos could forage for wild fruits such as dates, marulas, *stamvrug* (wild plums) and wild oranges.

Sugar, salt and spice supplies dwindled quickly. Cordials and honey became sugar substitutes; in place of salt, the Boers sometimes strapped raw meat to their horses' bodies so that the salt from the animals' sweat could permeate the meat before it was cooked. Meat was sometimes also grilled directly on the coals, which gave it a slightly salty taste.

The scorched-earth policy deprived the Boers of the farms that had acted as their supply depots, however, compelling them to attack and plunder British supply columns and supply trains. These actions would yield tinned food from as far afield as the United States, Argentina, Australia and Canada. The burghers would be particularly heartened if they could lay their hands on a sweet treat such as tinned plum pudding, chocolate, golden syrup or condensed milk.

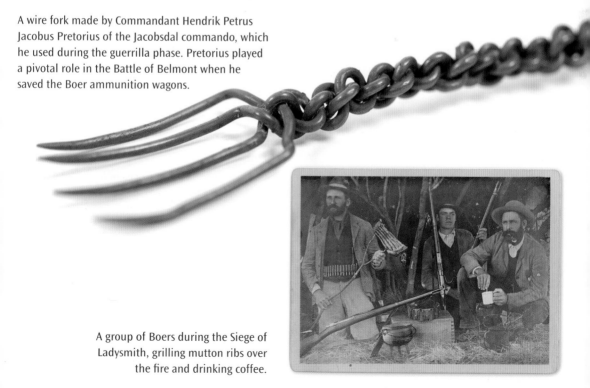

A wire fork made by Commandant Hendrik Petrus Jacobus Pretorius of the Jacobsdal commando, which he used during the guerrilla phase. Pretorius played a pivotal role in the Battle of Belmont when he saved the Boer ammunition wagons.

A group of Boers during the Siege of Ladysmith, grilling mutton ribs over the fire and drinking coffee.

Trusty Steeds

by Dané Swanepoel

The Anglo-Boer War had a huge impact not only on the people who lived in the republics and colonies, but also on their animals. It is estimated that the Boers lost 100 000 horses in battle, with the British losing three times that number.

The Boer horse, raised in the veld, had remarkably powerful limbs and tough hooves. Added to this, the Boers were regarded as proficient horsemen who had a deep understanding of their horses' needs. They also taught their horses to stand still while being dismounted, whereas British soldiers needed help with this. In the Boer commandos, the role of the black grooms in caring for horses was an important one. The grooms were also responsible for the pack horses, which carried the commando's blankets, food and cooking utensils.

During the guerrilla phase, part of the focus of Britain's scorched-earth policy involved the plundering or slaughter of the horses on Boer farms. British soldiers shot countless breeding mares and young horses in camps and in the field.

The British army imported horses from Australia, Argentina, Canada, Hungary, Italy and the United States, offloading them at Cape Town, Port Elizabeth and East London harbours, and transporting them to the front lines by rail. Many horses died at sea or shortly after making landfall, having been given far too little time to rest and acclimatise after the long voyage.

These imported horses were unprepared for the conditions they would face in the field, and were no match for the Boer horses. Many British soldiers could not ride, learning as they went; they often overloaded their animals, weakening and exhausting them.

British horses at a horse depot. The Wiltshire Regiment's horse depot was at the foot of Naval Hill in Bloemfontein. This depot was easy for the soldiers to find: on the slope of the hill, the shape of a large white horse had been laid out in stones. The white horse is still visible today.

Caltrops, such as the one shown at left, were strewn around the blockhouses to injure Boer horses, thereby preventing the Boers from breaking through the blockhouse lines. 🔫

The bit shown below also dates back to the war.

The food shortage during the siege of Ladysmith forced the British army to take the drastic step of slaughtering some of its horses. A concentrated paste made from horse flesh was mixed with water and served as soup, to the sick and wounded in particular. The paste was named 'Chevril', after Bovril. Horsemeat apparently made tasty sausage and biltong too.

A monument to all the horses that served, and died, in the British army during the war was unveiled at Port Elizabeth in 1905.

Names of well-known Boer generals' horses:
General Louis Botha: Dapper and Bles
General Koos de la Rey: Bokkie
General de Villebois-Mareuil: Colenso
General Christiaan de Wet: Fleur and Dapper
General Wynand Malan: Very Nice
General Jan Smuts: Charlie
General Ben Viljoen: Blesman
President MT Steyn: Scot

Have a Smoke

by Dané Swanepoel

For Boer and Brit alike, having a smoke was a popular way of whiling away leisure time. There are scores of photos showing Boer fighters on commando smoking together companionably, pipe in hand in place of expensive cigars or cigarettes.

At the start of the war, *De Volksstem*, a Transvaal newspaper, established a tobacco fund for burghers in the field. Paul Kruger was the first to contribute to the fund. With their parents' permission, Boer boys could start smoking at the age of 16.

A similar fund was established for British soldiers. Each Scottish soldier, for example, received a tin of tobacco as a New Year's gift. It was generally easier for British soldiers to get hold of tobacco than it was for the Boers.

The British could choose from a range of cigarette brands, such as Player's, Woodbine and Krüger. Krüger cigarettes were a Spanish brand that had Paul Kruger's face on the packet. Soldiers who smoked this brand were, effectively, smoking the enemy!

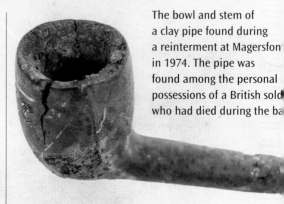

The bowl and stem of a clay pipe found during a reinterment at Magersfon in 1974. The pipe was found among the personal possessions of a British sold who had died during the ba

Tobacco grew progressively scarcer as the war went on, forcing the Boers to use their ingenuity to find alternatives. Some smoked hessian bags that had been soaked in sheep dip (the dip was made of tobacco extract); the more desperate smoked horse or cow droppings, pumpkin, peach and potato leaves, and even some roots and weeds.

Leather and hide tobacco pouches held the day's tobacco, but many Boers also owned pouches made of finer fabrics that their wives had decorated.

The Boer preference was for the wooden pipe, known as the briar or calabash pipe. They also smoked home-made pipes made from the shells of rifle rounds, wood and stone. Boer prisoners of war made pipes to while away the time and earn extra income. Some of these pipes featured artful engravings and even inlays.

Matches were already available during the war, in brand names such as Lion, Firefly and Commando. The Zuid-Afrikaansche Vuurhoutje Maatschappij manufactured Commando matches. Later in the war, matches were no longer available, and the men returned to the old-fashioned tinderbox and flint.

It did not take British business long to profit from the war. This cigarette advertisement, showing General Redvers Buller, appeared in the magazine *Navy & Army Illustrated* in December 1899.

Krüger cigarettes were manufactured in Spain out of sympathy for the Boer cause and are still made today. British soldiers usually bought them in Las Palmas, in the Canary Islands, on their way to South Africa. 🜚

The Tide Turns

In the war's final months, the two republics effectively became one big military camp. Thousands of troops were on the move in different columns; the dust trails of heavy military convoys crisscrossed the land. Hundreds of blockhouses stood sentry, and armoured trains patrolled between them.

The mighty British Empire was anxious to end the costly war. For months, however, a group of about 20 000 Bittereinders frustrated British efforts, stubbornly fighting on. The Bittereinders' faith, shared suffering and fears for their families, many of whom were in the concentration camps, deepened their determination to fight to the bitter end for their republics' independence. Leaders such as Louis Botha, Christiaan de Wet and Koos de la Rey urged them on.

Over and above the daily threat to their lives, the burghers in the field were desperately short of the most basic essentials, such as food and clothing. It was only in De la Rey's western Transvaal that the burghers' basic needs were met. Attacks on British convoys and the occasional skirmish with troops saw Bittereinders frequently fed, armed and even clothed courtesy of the British army supply depots.

The British military authorities resorted to increasingly drastic actions. In addition to a surge in the numbers of armed black men in British service, it took to using black groups to attack Boer fighters in the northern and eastern Transvaal and drive them out of those regions. For example, a group comprising Zulu fighters and a few burghers killed a commando at Holkrans, near Vryheid.

The republics may still have scored sporadic defeats against the British in battles such as the one at Ysterspruit, but the end of the war was near at hand. The situation in the Orange Free State was more of a concern: the commandos still engaged in frequent skirmishes, but the British columns and blockhouse lines kept the imperialists firmly in control.

In an attempt to relieve the pressure on the republics, General Jan Smuts and his commando embarked on an expedition deep into the Cape Colony in September 1901. He hoped to find citizens there whom he could recruit to join his commando as rebels. But the British were hot on his heels. He divided his beleaguered commando into four groups, and even made an attempt to besiege the copper-mining town of Okiep.

At the dawn of 1902, many Bittereinders started to question whether their fight would see the year out. Britain's raids and blockhouse lines, as well as its mounted infantry, were relentlessly eroding the effectiveness of the commando as a fighting force.

OPPOSITE A uniform made from the canvas canopy of a supply wagon. It belonged to burgher Gerhardus Jacobus Oosthuizen, a Bittereinder and member of the Krugersdorp commando. He was wounded at Peters Hill in Natal at the beginning of the war. Britain's scorched-earth policy forced the Bittereinders to find innovative solutions to meet their basic needs. By the end of the war, burghers were often seen in clothing made of sacking, carpets, curtains and wagon canopies. ✠

The Bloemfontein concentration camp,
with Spitskop in the background.

CHAPTER 8

Scorched Earth

Fire!

When Bloemfontein and Pretoria fell in 1900, the British government assumed – and hoped – that the republics would capitulate. It soon became clear, however, that this would not occur.

After the fall of Bloemfontein in March, Boer leaders convened a war council and decided that the republics would continue the fight. They would shift to guerrilla tactics and use small, mobile units to attack British supply columns and target the enemy's lines of communication.

In keeping with the stipulations of the Hague Convention of 1899, British forces had largely left the civilian populations in towns and on farms in peace after the Orange Free State had fallen – aside, of course, from confiscating horses and feed. However, a series of acts of sabotage, including General Christiaan de Wet's destruction of the British ammunition stockpile at Roodewal station, soon prodded Lord Roberts

into action. He issued a proclamation on 16 June 1900 warning the commandos that should they damage infrastructure such as bridges, telegraph lines, railway lines and tunnels, Britain would retaliate by razing the farmsteads nearest to the sites of sabotage.

So began Britain's scorched-earth policy. It contravened the Hague Convention, compelling President MT Steyn to raise strong objections to it in several letters to Lord Roberts.

By the time Lord Kitchener assumed command of British forces in South Africa at the end of November 1900, the guerrilla phase of the war was already in full swing. Kitchener came under huge pressure from the British government to end the war – after all, it was costing the British taxpayer £2.5 million per month. It was time to take drastic measures.

It did not take long for Kitchener to realise that every farm in the two republics served a range

British troops at a burnt-out farmhouse.
The location of the farmhouse is unknown.
Western Cape Archives

A mantel clock that remained intact, aside from some light fire damage to the decorative elements on its left-hand side, after a farmhouse in Kleinsmaldeel, in the Winburg district, was razed.

of purposes: they stockpiled supplies, relayed information and soothed the burghers' souls. The women on the farms were behind these support structures, supplying food and encouraging the men to keep fighting.

Kitchener devised a three-pronged strategy. First, Roberts's proclamation about the destruction of farmsteads would be implemented with greater vigour and even expanded. This would sever connections between the Bittereinders ('bitter enders') and their support systems. Roberts had issued a more draconian proclamation in September 1900, which decreed that all property within a 16-km radius of an act of sabotage would be destroyed. Second, the refugee camps, established largely for hensoppers ('hands-uppers') in Bloemfontein and Pretoria, would become concentration camps that could also house the women and children removed from the burnt-out farms. Third, the blockhouse system would be rolled out to capture the commandos in large-scale raids.

This began the process that would burn down 30 000 farmhouses, lay waste to harvests, break dams, kill thousands of cattle and destroy 40 towns, partially or fully, in the two republics. Buildings were burnt or dynamited. Bothaville, Ventersburg and Lindley in the Orange Free State, and Ermelo in the Transvaal, are all examples of towns that were completely destroyed as a result of the scorched-earth policy.

A Broadwood piano that belonged to burgher FN Joubert of the farm Fonteintjie, near Colesberg. British soldiers spent a night on the farm and threw a party in the farmhouse, stubbing their cigarettes out on the piano to leave burn marks that are still visible today. Broadwood pianos were manufactured in Britain by a family firm founded by the grandfather of General Robert George Broadwood, who was defeated at the Battle of Sannaspos.

A silver tea and coffee set that was hidden in a stone wall on a farm near Philippolis.

A well-known eyewitness reports

In a letter to President MT Steyn, General Jan Smuts, Transvaal attorney general and, later, prime minister of the Union of South Africa, described the effects of the scorched-earth policy on a region between the Magaliesberg and Witwatersberg (in the Krugersdorp district) as follows:

A Boer woman and her family turn away from the camera as their home goes up in flames.

Allow me to give an example of a specific area … one of the most fertile and best-cultivated areas in South Africa. When I came to the area in July 1900, it was green, with uninterrupted and well-cultivated fields, flower and vegetable gardens, beautiful homes and farmsteads – a real treat for the eye and evidence of what our people had achieved agriculturally in the span of a few decades.

But now! Today, it is a devastated, barren wilderness – all the fields have been destroyed, the trees in the gardens chopped down or torn out of the ground, the houses burnt down, completely destroyed, in many cases, by dynamite so that not one stone is left stacked upon another. They now shelter only the owl and other night creatures.

Where once life, prosperity and excitement reigned, now only death prevails. Not a single living animal, woman, child, or even black woman is to be seen without fear, hunger, misery and despair on its face.

Surviving in the Field

As in almost every war before it and since, the Anglo-Boer War caused extreme suffering among the civilian population. The families of the burghers on commando were the hardest hit: with the men commandeered, it fell to the women and older children to meet the daily management obligations on the farms.

A skirt made of sacking, hemmed with black mourning bands. It was made by one Mrs Fourie of the Bethlehem district, whose house was razed before she could save any of her possessions. While on the run in the veld, she learnt that her husband had died, hence the mourning bands. 🔫

Scores of Boer women stayed behind on the farms, but, as the scorched-earth policy became more strictly enforced, this became increasingly dangerous. Many women chose to come together in encampments to evade capture and escape detention in concentration camps. For protection, these encampments stayed close to commandos. The gatherings comprised anything from five to over 200 carriages of all kinds, from ox-wagons to spiders (light, four-wheeled horse-drawn carriages), *bokkiekarre* (open, two-wheeled horse-drawn carriages) and Cape carts (two-wheeled horse-drawn carriages with covered tops).

The women's encampments had advantages and disadvantages. On the one hand, moving with a commando provided protection, food and information about enemy movements. On the other, however, the women tended to move with thousands of head of livestock, which reduced their mobility considerably.

When the British captured the encampments, they burned most of the women's possessions, save for a few carriages, and killed their livestock. When the commandos tried to relieve a captured encampment, British soldiers would sometimes encircle themselves with the Boer families, whom they had forced onto their carriages. Using the women and children as cover, the British would then fire on the commandos from within a circle of women.

Many women chose to go it alone, eking out an existence with their families in the bush. General Koos de la Rey's wife, Nonnie, is perhaps the best-known example of this: she sought to avoid capture and internment in a concentration camp at all costs.

The topography of the two republics often dictated the women's movements. Women in the eastern Orange Free State, for example, sheltered in caves, and women in the eastern Transvaal

Many Boer women left their farms with their families and joined so-called women's encampments, as depicted in this photo.

RIGHT A shortage of horses meant that fleeing women and children often had to use cattle to pull horse carts.

took advantage of the mountainous and bushy landscape. It became increasingly difficult, however, for women to stay on the run as the war progressed and British flames consumed more farms.

Catharina Venter of the Fauresmith district fled her home on 30 April 1901. In the book *Die Helde-album*, she speaks of her experiences: 'We fled with thirteen carriages and six wagons, and had two hundred horses and cows and about three thousand sheep with us. After only a few hours, we suddenly spotted a battle ahead of us … we hurried away and stopped at a pan near Modder River.

'Mrs Casper Venter was in pain. We took her through a ford to an abandoned house where she gave birth to a baby girl. After fifteen days next to the river, we pushed on over rocks and bushes where no road had ever been, because the enemy was all around us.

'The baby fell sick and died on the same day. We buried her in the veld and raced towards Kimberley.'

During the peace negotiations at Vereeniging, General Louis Botha estimated that 2 540 families remained in the field.

Jurgens Nieman's Story

Hundreds of Boer women fled with their children into the veld during the war. Rumours about the concentration camps heightened their tension whenever British columns or patrols came near.

Mrs Hansie Breytenback recorded Jurgens Albertus Nieman's story. Her mother was Susara Susanna Nieman, Jurgens' older sister:

Jurgens Albertus Nieman was born on 10 December 1898. At 08h00 on 27 July 1900, a bullet from the rifle of an English soldier hit him in the head in the Witpoort area in the western Transvaal. He died at 20h00 that same evening.

Jurgens was the son of the scout Jurgens Albertus Nieman, who was never captured or wounded … He and his 14-year-old son Jacobus Johannes fled the siege and surrender of General Piet Cronjé (Battle of Paardeberg) on a young horse – with neither saddle nor bridle.

Jurgens' mother was Anna Elizabeth. She and the four other children fled the English forces on a horse-drawn cart. A trusted black worker fled with them, and they took a small herd of sheep with them too.

On 26 July 1900 they were caught and loaded onto an open ox-wagon and taken to the Klerksdorp concentration camp. Other wagons joined them and they had to spend the night in the open veld. At about 08h00 on the morning of 27 July, the mother and smaller children walked over to another wagon to become better acquainted.

Suddenly, Jurgens started to fidget and become bothersome. When his mother picked him up and pressed his head to her chest, blood trickled down her hands. She discovered that he had been shot in the head. They had heard the English shooting in the distance; a 'stray' bullet must have struck him. Jurgens died at 20h00 that night.

These are the clothes he was wearing that day. The two bullet wounds and the blood stain are clearly visible in the bonnet. (The worst of the blood has been washed out.)

Jurgens was buried in a shallow grave at the side of the road. His name and other details were written on a little plank and planted at the grave. His father and other scouts came upon the grave fourteen days later. The cold had kept the child's body almost perfectly preserved and recognisable. He placed the little casket in front of him on his horse and took it to Rustfontein farm, where the child was buried.

The slate gravestone of Jurgens Albertus Nieman.

The bonnet, dress and shoes that Jurgens Nieman was wearing when he was hit by a stray bullet. One hole is clearly visible (circled). Boys of three years and younger were often dressed as girls in the Victorian era, so it was not unusual to see boys in bonnets and dresses. The dress was made from a scarf belonging to his 17-year-old sister, Susara Susanna.

A British Soldier's Story

British officer CR Ballard's version of the events that unfolded when his patrol captured a women's encampment on 12 June 1901 and a Boer girl was fatally wounded:

We have not had anything of a fight for two months and I have quite forgotten what it is to be under fire – but we captured a good many wagons, mostly full of women and children. We had a horrible accident which upset me for a time – we shot a little girl – it was horrible.

Of course it was an accident; we were chasing some wagons and instead of pulling up to show they gave in, some of the people jumped out and hid in a little wooden glen by the road side – I suppose our men could not see clearly so they let them fly on chance and hit a girl. She was mortally wounded.

She was quite a pretty little girl about ten years old and full of pluck. She kept on saying, "I am alright aunt, and I don't think the English have caught the wagons – oh I hope they won't catch the wagons". I would have given anything for the wagons to get away then – but unfortunately they were caught and when she saw them turned around and coming back she broke down and began to cry.

We had no doctor, but the doctor who saw her later told me she must have been in awful pain as she was internally injured – she died early next morning and had a military funeral before we started.

I am nervous that we may hit some more people if we go on like this, for we've got a long-range Elswick gun and whenever a wagon is seen in the far distance, we shell it, and it is generally full of women and children.

– As quoted in *Suffering of War*

Elizabeth (Lily) Maré was a young woman when her family's town house in Middelburg was commandeered by Major General Reginald Pole-Carew. The incessant mewing by Lily's cat kept the general from his sleep and consequently one of his soldiers killed the animal. A distraught Lily apparently reprimanded the general. In November 1900, she received a letter from Pole-Carew in which he apologised for having had her cat killed and also sent her this brooch.

The Perseverance of Kotie Steenkamp

What Boer woman Kotie Steenkamp endured during the Anglo-Boer War was not hers alone to suffer; scores of other women shared her experiences. Her daughter Johanna recalled her story to Rev. JP Jacobs, Johanna's husband, who recorded it in writing.

Kotie Steenkamp before the war.

The Steenkamps farmed on Duplessisdam, the family farm in the Boshof district. When war broke out, Kotie's husband joined the Boshof commando, participating in the battles and sieges on the western border of the Orange Free State. He was captured at Paardeberg and exiled to St Helena.

Kotie's story opens with a description of how she, a woman alone, had to manage the farm in the first phase of the war, shearing sheep and tending the livestock in addition to her household tasks. As the war ground on, it increasingly affected the Steenkamp family. It started with British forces confiscating some of their livestock; the next thing she knew, she was preparing for a nomadic life and hiding her most precious possessions. Kotie fled to a women's encampment with the family's remaining livestock, which a farm worker herded. When the worst of the danger had passed, she returned to the farm.

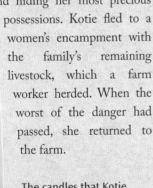

The candles that Kotie Steenkamp had with her during her itinerant years. Items such as candles and soap were a luxury for most women in Kotie's situation; they were made of animal fat, and livestock was scarce.

When a British column inevitably razed the Duplessisdam farmstead, the Steenkamp family spent the rest of the war in the veld with their spring-wagon, remaining sheep, two horses and three chickens. Kotie knew all too well how defenceless the large women's encampments were, choosing to go it alone instead. In time, her little herd became tamer, which made it easier for the family to move around.

Her readiness and diligence is evident in her daughter's description of how everything had its specific place in the spring-wagon; it was too dangerous to use a lamp to find things at night, as this might attract the attention of the enemy.

Essentials such as fabric soon ran short. When the family's clothing wore out, Johanna explains, Kotie would 'first boil the sheets in elandsboontjie water and then dip them in cold lime water, so that they had a pleasant brown colour, and then make dresses from them'. Kotie even made shoes for the burghers and supplied them with tobacco, which she made by drying camphor bush leaves and dipping them in tobacco extract.

Time and again, Kotie evaded capture, despite the fact that there were 16 British columns crisscrossing the Boshof district in the middle of 1901 to hunt down the remaining commandos and nomadic families. The family did have a few narrow escapes, however: during one, a mounted column surprised Kotie and her children on a farm she was visiting. As a preventive measure, the British captured Abraham, her oldest son (aged just 14), and sent him with a group of other young boys as prisoners of war to Bermuda.

Unusually, the Steenkamp family was reunited after the war; they were one of the few families not to have lost a single member.

The Concentration Camps

Shortly after occupying Bloemfontein in March 1900, British military authorities established a refugee camp to protect republican burghers who had laid down their weapons. The scorched-earth policy, which commenced in June 1900, displaced large numbers of women and children, who also needed to be accommodated somewhere. So, the Bloemfontein refugee camp became a concentration camp in September 1900.

Spanish general Valeriano Weyler had set up the first concentration camps, in Cuba in 1896, in an active attempt to depopulate outlying areas of the island. Over 200 000 Cubans died in the camps as a result of disease and starvation.

In the Boer republics, white and black women and children from the farms that the British had destroyed were taken to the camps by train and ox-wagon; for convenience, the camps were often built near main rail lines. Over a span of five months, many camps were established in the Transvaal and Orange Free State to cope with the increasing numbers of people who had been displaced by the scorched-earth policy.

That British military authorities were underprepared for the concentration camp system was clear from the overcrowding in many of the camps and from the desperate shortages of essential commodities. Winter and summer, families were housed in old, badly worn bell tents; in the Springfontein camp, up to 20 people lived in tents meant for six.

Food, clean water, clothes, wood, beds and mattresses were inadequate. Toilet facilities – no more than ditches overlaid with logs and partitioned with corrugated-iron sheeting – were a breeding ground for disease. Inadequate sanitation and general deprivation quickly led to outbreaks of disease, which led, in turn, to widespread deaths.

In addition to the camps for white women and children, camps were established for black civilians, who had also largely come from farms. Residents of these camps had to see to their own food and shelter: British authorities reasoned that the war was not being waged against them in particular, and that they were also free to earn an income by working for the British army.

Women and children walk towards a concentration camp at Pietersburg.

'The black spot – the one very black spot – in the picture
is the frightful mortality in the concentration camps.
I entirely agree with you in the thinking that while
a hundred explanations may be offered and a hundred excuses
made, they do not really amount to an adequate defence.'
– Sir Alfred Milner, in a letter to Joseph Chamberlain, Secretary of State for
Colonies, as quoted in *Verskroeide Aarde*

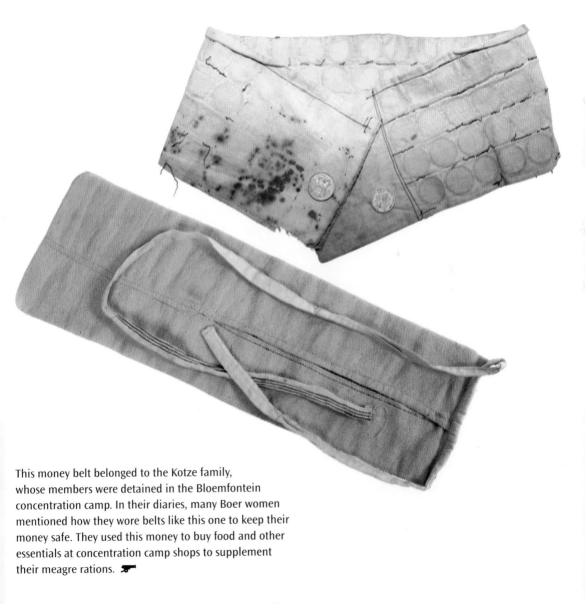

This money belt belonged to the Kotze family,
whose members were detained in the Bloemfontein
concentration camp. In their diaries, many Boer women
mentioned how they wore belts like this one to keep their
money safe. They used this money to buy food and other
essentials at concentration camp shops to supplement
their meagre rations.

The need for a reliable labour force saw these camps being placed, in the middle of 1901, in the hands of the Native Refugee Department under Captain GF de Lotbinière.

Later, camp schools were established, with classes given by English-speaking teachers. Ministers were also permitted to give spiritual counsel, but only those whom military authorities had endorsed.

After her first visit to the camps in April and May 1901, British humanitarian Emily Hobhouse compiled a comprehensive report on them and distributed it in Britain. Public reaction to Hobhouse's report pressured the British government to establish the Fawcett Commission, tasked with making recommendations for improving camp conditions.

By August 1901, almost 94 000 women and children languished in the white camps. In what became known as Black October in 1901, 1 520 of these died as a result of abysmal living conditions. In the end, over 26 379 of the estimated 150 000 detainees in the 47 white camps died. (Research by Celeste Reynolds in the early 2000s places the death toll in the white camps at close to 34 000, but this includes deaths in transit to the camps.) The vast majority of deaths – 22 057 – occurred among children under 16 years of age.

About 140 000 black people were sent to the black camps in the two republics. A practically equal number of deaths – about 24 000 – was recorded in the 65 black camps.

The trauma of the concentration camps would linger in the Afrikaner psyche and worldview for generations to come.

A bonnet that belonged to Mrs H Venter, detained in the Springfontein camp. On receiving the news that her husband had died, she stitched the crêpe onto the bonnet, crêpe being a symbol of mourning in the Victorian era.

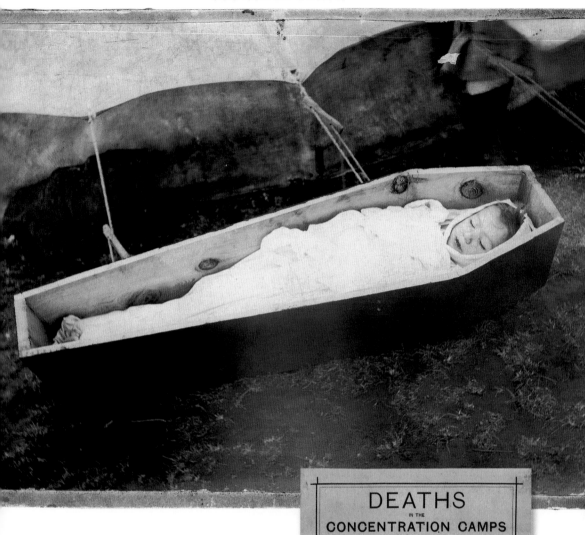

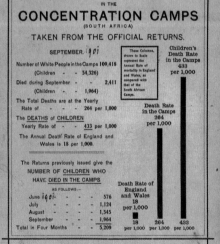

ABOVE and **BELOW** Japie Bergh died in the Bloemfontein concentration camp at age three. On his deathbed he gave this screw to his mother to hand to his father after he returned from commando.

RIGHT A notice that was published in Britain about the deaths in the concentration camps.

Camp Rations

Malnutrition was an inevitable result of the meagre rations provided in the concentration camps. Small children suffered the worst effects; scores died of nutrition-related diseases. When a family arrived at a camp, its size was noted and a ration card issued to the head of the family. The card specified the exact quantities of food to be issued to each person.

Until March 1901 – and later, in some cases – ration scales distinguished between two types of Boer families: those whose men were still on commando, and those whose men had laid down their weapons. The scales discriminated against the former, allocating them smaller portions. This practice was particularly common in the Transvaal camps.

Rations comprised basic foodstuffs such as flour, sugar, coffee, salt, condensed milk and meat. Luxuries such as soap were excluded. To satisfy their eternal hunger, some of the children foraged for veld food such as *uintjies* (a type of edible corm), *brakvye* (the fruits of mesembryanthemum plants) and wild asparagus roots. Vegetables were a rare exception, and items such as milk were reserved – if available at all – for camp hospitals and infants. What little livestock remained was in such poor condition that the meat it yielded was often inedible. Quality aside, sometimes meat that had already started to rot was handed out; in many cases, doctors condemned the meat rations

This frame was made by Mrs CM Roos of Heilbron after the war, using labels from tins of corned meat or bully beef. Corned meat was part of camp residents' rations. In the top left corner are several staples, extracted from the contents of the tins. These staples made their way into the tins due to poor manufacturing practices. Another theory holds that the tinned meat was manufactured in an American factory that employed many Irish workers, and that these workers intentionally slipped the staples into the meat.

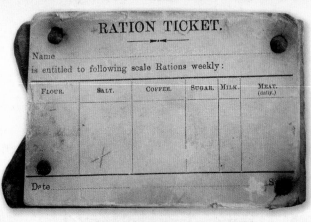

as unfit for human consumption. To make matters worse, the supply of wood for cooking fires was inadequate.

When livestock shortages hit in September 1901, rations were supplemented with tins of corned meat or bully beef. Towards the end of the war, frozen meat was imported from Australia; the supply contract for the Orange Free State camps was awarded to Champion & Co's Cold Storage Company. Meat supplies were unreliable, however, due to the long distances they had to travel to reach the camps.

In the wake of the Fawcett Commission's camp visits, several recommendations were made to improve camp rations. The Commission was especially concerned about the high mortality rate among children under five, which was ascribed to poor diet: the malnourished children had no resistance to disease.

A ration card for six adults and one child. The card was issued to JN van Reenen in the Ladysmith concentration camp. Also known as 'Tin Town', this camp was primarily a transit camp; many prisoners of war were detained here en route to other camps.

Ration scales for under-fives were revised in January 1902. The new scales made provision for milk, flour, oats, sugar, syrup, butter, salt, soap and vegetables. Whereas not all of these items were available all the time, the ration improvements did lead to a decline in mortality rates.

Later in the war, shops were permitted in the camps. However, most detainees by then had no money to spend in them.

Meat rations for distribution among hensoppers in the Springfontein concentration camp.

Marbles and Dolls

by Dané Swanepoel

The suffering in the camps aside, children will be children. Nothing could stand between them and playtime – when their chores were done, of course. Girls usually helped their mothers with washing and boys took care of water, firewood and collecting rations.

Many mothers made ragdolls for their daughters to make camp life a little more bearable. Others brought their daughters' porcelain dolls with them. These so-called China dolls had a head and shoulders of glazed porcelain and a leather or fabric body, stuffed with sawdust. The doll's limbs were also made of leather, fabric or porcelain. Frozen Charlotte or penny dolls were solid porcelain dolls, with painted-on faces and hair.

According to *Kampkinders 1900–1902: 'n Gedenkboek*, boys came together to play in small groups. Popular games included football, using a tin as a ball, *kennetjie* (a game played with sticks), *blikaspaai* (a modified 'I spy' game) and horseshoe throwing. But, the most popular game was marbles, a game for up to six players. Each marble type was assigned a name and a value. 'Pitte' were brown or dull marbles, likely unglazed clay marbles; 'lemmies' were the marbles found in lemonade bottles; and 'glasies' (glassies) were the glass balls found in bottles of soda water, ginger beer and lemonade. (Marbles were placed in soft drink bottles to prevent the gas from escaping from the bottle; the gas would push the marble into the neck of the bottle, forming an airtight seal.)

A ragdoll made by one Mrs Piek for her daughter in the Heilbron concentration camp. It is one of only two that still exist. ✄

A little girl with a ragdoll in the Colenso concentration camp.

On a player's good days, he would win many marbles; on less auspicious ones, he would need to ask his friends for a few *pitte*. To do this, he would have to make a fist so that his friend could shoot his knuckles hard with the marble – the price to pay for readmission to the game. Losing an 'ironie', likely a metal marble, was a real misfortune, as was a *glasie* breaking. When this happened, the boys would have to hope that they would find a soda water bottle lying around soon.

Playing marbles was Boer boys' favourite pastime. They would often break lemonade bottles such as this one to get to the glass ball inside. These bottles were excavated near the Bloemfontein concentration camp; the glass marble belonged to a boy in the Norvalspont camp. The pouch of marbles belonged to Johannes Gerhardus Bester Fourie of Bethlehem, detained with his family in the Bloemfontein concentration camp.

Sickness and Medical Care

The concentration camps inflicted great physical and spiritual trauma on all who were sent to them. The journey to the camps alone was an ordeal. Some were transported by ox-wagon on a journey that could take up to three or four days. Others were taken to assembly points along a railway line, then loaded onto open train carriages for a journey to the nearest camp, which could take as long as three days.

Scores, then, arrived at the camps already traumatised, starving, dirty and, often, sick. The tents to which they were allocated were badly worn and often already overcrowded. The camps themselves were too small for the numbers of people they had to accommodate; overcrowding encouraged the spread of disease, especially among children under five.

It was hardly surprising, then, that one of the first disease outbreaks was dysentery – the result of poor sanitation and contaminated water. Pneumonia and bronchitis flourished during the winter months, claiming many of the elderly.

Lest we forget

A plaque commemorating Anna Magdalena Booysen, born on 8 February 1899 in the Waterberg. She died of dysentery on 26 November 1901 in the Nylstroom concentration camp. Similar metal plaques, shaped like hearts or flowers, appeared on many graves during the war. The name of the deceased was hammered into the plaque with a small nail.

In areas where sandstone or slate was available, small gravestones were made and the names of loved ones engraved on them with wire or nails. Other graves were marked with sealed bottles containing the names of the deceased written on pieces of paper.

The photograph above, taken shortly after the war, shows Annie Grové of Lydenburg, her husband and their son at their daughter Wilhelmina's grave. Wilhelmina died of measles, aged one year and seven months, in the Barberton concentration camp.

Elisa Monamoli's gravestone in what was once
Nooitgedacht, the black concentration camp at
Brandfort. Many black people were removed with their
employers from farms as part of the scorched-earth policy, but scores
were also taken from their own homes and mission stations. Record-
keeping in the black camps was poor, but an estimated 24 000 black
people are thought to have died there. 🔫

Some detainees hailed from remote rural areas, and had never been exposed to diseases such as measles. This lack of immunity led to countless deaths.

The camp hospitals lacked adequate medical staff, medicines and equipment. Their high mortality rates, and the indifferent treatment by some of the staff, made them much-feared; residents believed that their relatives stood a better chance of recovery in their own tents, being cared for by their own families. However, the British doctors regarded traditional medicines and Boer remedies as backward; to prevent disease from spreading, they ordered all sick residents to be treated in the camp hospital – and to be taken there by force, if necessary.

Mortality rates were high, especially between August and November 1901. It was not uncommon, in some camps, for 20 funerals to be held in a single day – a source of great embarrassment for the British government. When a camp resident died, the body was taken to a mortuary tent and had to be buried within a day or two. Up to three people would be buried in one grave. The shortage of wood saw soap and candle crates being repurposed as caskets, most often for children. Alternatively, the remains of loved ones were simply wrapped in khaki-coloured blankets – similar to those issued to British soldiers. Most families found this very traumatic.

The Fawcett Commission, which travelled to South Africa in 1901 to investigate camp conditions, made recommendations for improving medical care in the camps. One of these was that camp hospitals had to be better staffed, and that rations for camp residents had to include more nourishing food such as milk, butter and vegetables.

Camp residents were later recruited to work in the hospitals for a small wage, and additional British nursing staff and doctors were recruited to the camps in the last six months of the war. This, along with improved rations, reduced the spread of disease.

A chest displaying the Red Cross emblem, the property of Mrs Elizabeth Hendrina van den Heever. A doctor at the Winburg camp hospital gave it to her.

Through the eyes of a nurse

To earn a little extra money, many Boer women went to work as hospital assistants, although the pay was very low. Sarie Roos, one of the few qualified Afrikaans nurses, and who worked in the Bethulie concentration camp, described her experiences there in her diary:

Until now, August, we have had almost only dysentery ['koors'] in the camp. But measles have now broken out and the doctor has told me that 400 cases were reported this morning. There are too many patients for the hospital, so they have to stay in the tents.

This ordeal was surely too awful for words. For one thing, the sick people mostly slept on the floor. Few had the privilege of lying on a bed. In addition, we had lots of rain and everyone knows that measles do not like the cold and damp.

O! To crown the wretchedness, the people in the camp were without candles and without matches – martial law, no light must shine in the camp, because the burghers would see it. I am not exaggerating when I say that one has to feel, in the dark, whether the sick are still alive or have already gone cold …

The camp is divided into rows and each line has a corporal and a nurse. It makes the work easier; the nurse goes from tent to tent every day to track down the sick. If someone looks poorly, the temperature is taken, and if it is not satisfactory, a report is made and sent to the hospital. The public who are so scared of the hospital hid the first to take ill until the last. Believe me, the stretcher is placed before the bed, the patient is lifted onto it without a single groan.

Staff of the Barberton
concentration camp hospital.

A symbol of suffering

This photograph of seven-year-old Lizzie van Zyl, taken in the Bloemfontein concentration camp and passed on to the British press by Emily Hobhouse, led to widespread criticism of the British government's concentration camp system. The Van Zyls were the family of an 'undesirable', a republican burgher who had continued the fight, so the family was placed on one of the lowest ration scales. In this photograph, the emaciated Lizzie – who died in May 1901 – holds a doll that Hobhouse had given her.

The overwhelming reaction to the photograph in Britain saw Captain AG Trollope, superintendent of the Orange River Colony Refugee Camps, charged with investigating the circumstances under which she died. The head of the camp hospital alleged that Lizzie had arrived at the camp in her weakened state, and had worsened because of her own mother's neglect.

Hobhouse dismissed these allegations in the *Westminster Gazette* of 27 January 1902. She referred to the numerous witnesses who disputed Trollope's allegations, but whom the investigation never approached: 'One feels ashamed that any English journal, and English writer, should at such a moment impugn the conduct of distracted parents or drag a dead child into the public arena.

'Lizzie van Zyl will probably live in the annals of South Africa. She was one of the first batch of children who succumbed to the unnatural and now condemned system of reconcentration … Will it need the deaths of all the children to move the heart of England? At least in common decency we might cease reviling the Boer mothers, and stand aside in reverence while they mourn their dead.'

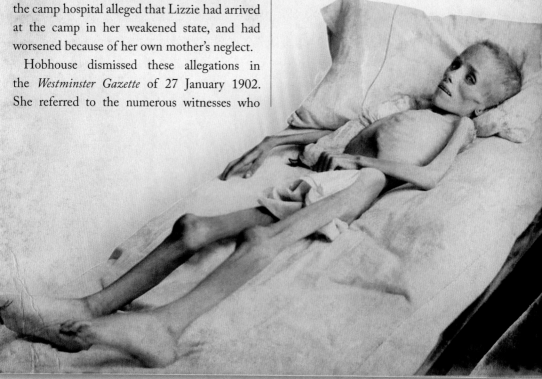

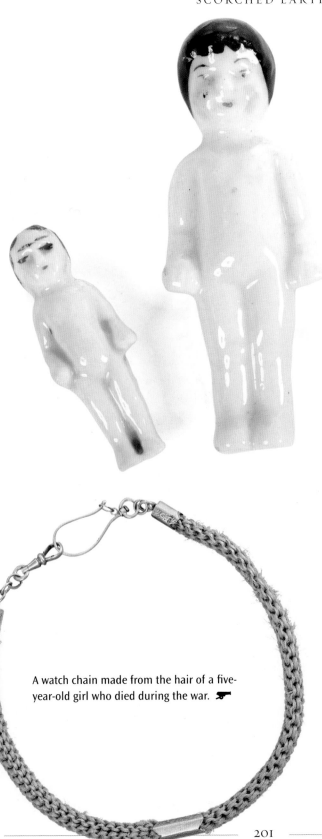

Many Boer children took so-called frozen Charlottes, or penny dolls, to the concentration camps. These porcelain dolls had painted faces and hair.

A watch chain made from the hair of a five-year-old girl who died during the war.

A sketch of the SS *Aurania* by a prisoner of war. The *Aurania* was a transport ship that departed Durban for Bombay (now Mumbai) on 21 September 1901, carrying a group of prisoners of war.

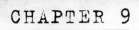

CHAPTER 9

British and Boer Prisoners of War

British POW Camps
October 1899–September 1900

The London Convention of 1884 between Britain and the South African Republic prohibited the Transvaal from signing any treaties or coming to any agreements with foreign states without Britain's approval. For this reason, the South African Republic was not a signatory to the Hague Convention of 1899. Still, the two Boer republics tried to apply the provisions of the Convention with regards to prisoners of war.

After the Boers took their first prisoners of war, at the Battle of Kraaipan, on 12 October 1899, they urgently had to make plans to house them somewhere. At that point neither the Orange Free State nor the Transvaal really had facilities to keep prisoners of war. After the battles in Natal in the first few months of the war, the need for an established prisoner-of-war camp became even greater. The Boer republics decided to send all prisoners of war to the South African Republic to hinder any effort by British forces to try and free them. One of the most famous British prisoners of war was the journalist Winston Churchill, who was captured at Chieveley, in Natal, at this time.

The number of prisoners of war increased dramatically after the Boer victories at Stormberg, Magersfontein and Colenso in December 1899. The British soldiers captured at Stormberg, for instance, were evacuated to Bloemfontein by rail and were kept in the cellars of the Railway Bureau (the building where the Bloemfontein Conference had taken place earlier that year) until the prisoner-of-war camps established in the Transvaal were ready to receive them.

The prisoner-of-war camp for British soldiers at Waterval, north of Pretoria.

VAN HOEPEN

As an interim measure, the South African Republic kept British officers at the Staats Model School in Pretoria until mid-March 1900, when they were taken to a camp near Fort Daspoort in the city. The officers soon dubbed the new camp 'The Birdcage'.

Non-commissioned officers and other ranks were held at Waterval, north of Pretoria, where the participants in the Jameson Raid of 1896 had also been interned. The camp had structures made of corrugated iron and was fenced off with barbed wire. It was lit up at night and well-guarded. British prisoners of war who were wounded or ill were treated at a hospital at the Pretoria racecourse.

Of course there were a number of escapes by British officers and soldiers. Apart from Churchill, Captain Aylmer Haldane, Lieutenant George le Mesurier and Sergeant Major A Brockie also escaped from the Staats Model School.

A day before British troops entered Pretoria (5 June 1900), the South African Republic evacuated about 900 prisoners of war to Nooitgedacht, east of Pretoria. However, the majority of prisoners – 148 officers and 3 041 men left behind in Pretoria – were relieved by Brigadier General TC Porter's brigade and the Royal Scots Greys.

On 30 August, 1 900 more British prisoners of war were freed, and in September 1900, General John French relieved the last men held in captivity (23 officers and 59 men), at Barberton.

October 1900–May 1902

During the guerrilla phase of the war, a completely different approach was followed to prisoners of wars, since the Boer commandos no longer had access to their capital cities and the necessary infrastructure.

British troops who fell into the hands of the Boers at this point were usually stripped of their uniforms, because the burghers' clothing was rather threadbare by then. The Boers called this process 'uitskud' (literally 'shake out'). The British soldiers were then released.

Another very famous British prisoner of war was Lord Methuen, who was injured and then captured by General Koos de la Rey in the Battle of Tweebosch (7 March 1902). Methuen's wounds were treated by a doctor, after which De la Rey's wife, Nonnie, prepared a meal for him. De la Rey then released Methuen. This incident was the start of a friendship between the two men that would last many years.

According to British sources, nearly 380 officers and about 9 000 troops were captured by the Boers during the war. About 100 died in captivity.

'Ladysmith Street' in the Waterval camp.

Boer POW Camps in South Africa

British forces captured the first prisoners of war – a group of 184 Boers – after the Battle of Elandslaagte. As a signatory to the Hague Convention of 1899, Britain was obligated to honour the clause determining that prisoners of war should be treated fairly and humanely.

It may have been easy to accommodate this small group on transport ships, but the need for alternatives quickly became critical: General Piet Cronjé surrendered – with 4 000 burghers – at Paardeberg at the end of February 1900, and, five months later, 4 400 men handed themselves over in the Brandwater Basin. British military authorities feared that the Boers would free these prisoners if they managed to invade the Cape Colony, so they opted to send them overseas.

As a temporary measure, four camps – Green Point (Cape Town), Bellevue (Simon's Town), Tin Town (Ladysmith) and Umbilo (Durban) – were hastily erected.

Most of the prisoners of war were housed in the Green Point camp, built on the site of the Green Point racecourse. Seven rows of 22 tents had to suffice in the small area; up to 12 men had to share tents made for six. The prisoners kept themselves busy by forming several societies, whose activities were frequently stalled, however, as transport ships became available and groups of prisoners were sent overseas.

Two rows of barbed wire encircled the Green Point camp. The area between the rows was a restricted area, or dead space. Guards were authorised summarily to shoot dead any prisoner

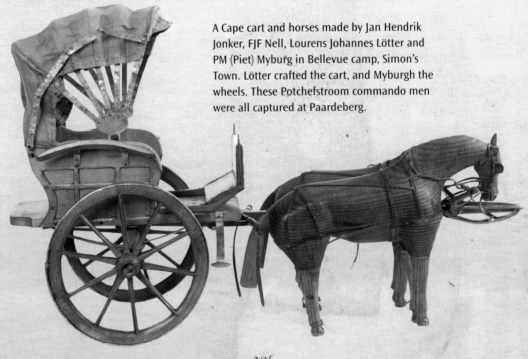

A Cape cart and horses made by Jan Hendrik Jonker, FJF Nell, Lourens Johannes Lötter and PM (Piet) Myburg in Bellevue camp, Simon's Town. Lötter crafted the cart, and Myburgh the wheels. These Potchefstroom commando men were all captured at Paardeberg.

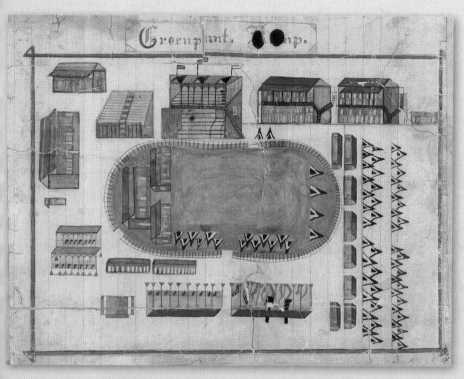

A watercolour of the Green Point camp, painted by a prisoner of war. It shows the stadium and a few temporary corrugated-iron buildings.

The Green Point prisoner-of-war camp. When the camp at the racecourse became too small, a second camp was erected beside it. The prisoners christened this camp Sky View: screened off by a fence of corrugated-iron sheeting, the camp offered views of only the blue sky and Table Mountain.

who strayed into this area. Guards patrolled an elevated wooden platform erected around the outer fence, and floodlights blazed in the camp at night. A third fence of horizontal iron bars was added to the camp's outer perimeter as a further precaution.

As prisoner-of-war numbers increased, an extension, Camp Number 2, was added to Green Point in September 1900. Troublemakers and recalcitrants (*onversoenlikes*: literally, 'those who would not reconcile'), in particular, were held there.

Bellevue, a second, fully fledged camp, was quickly erected at Simon's Town and put into operation in March 1900. Large numbers of prisoners of war were held on transport ships in Simon's Bay harbour as an interim measure while this camp was being constructed. Conditions on the ships were very poor. Over time, burghers who had taken the Oath of Neutrality were sent to Bellevue, where they remained until the end of the war. Those who refused the Oath were sent to Green Point, and on to camps overseas. Like Green Point, Bellevue was securely fenced and floodlit at night. Its prisoners were permitted to take dips in the ocean; during one such swimming session, a prisoner was taken by a shark.

Two camps went up in Natal. Durban's Umbilo camp was also a transit camp for prisoners of war who were destined for overseas camps, and Ladysmith's Tin Town camp was in an old corrugated-iron British barracks, where prisoners were housed from December 1900 onwards. Like Bellevue, Tin Town came, over time, to house prisoners who had taken the Oath.

When peace was concluded, on 31 May 1902, Tin Town and Bellevue served as temporary housing for returning prisoners of war. The other camps were closed down.

A *slangdosie* ('snake box') made by a Green Point prisoner of war for playing a trick on others. The snake in this instance had a sharp point on the front, which would prick the finger of the person who slid the lid open. ⚓

St Helena

St Helena, a mountainous island of deep ravines and precious little level ground, is located in the middle of the South Atlantic about 2 700 km from Cape Town. In 1900, it was home to 3 342 residents and a garrison of close to 1 800; a total of 5 860 prisoners of war would ultimately come to be held here.

On 5 April 1900, not long after the capitulation at Paardeberg, the first group of prisoners of war arrived at St Helena. The group numbered 514 Boers and 18 *agterryers*, or grooms, and included the first group of prisoners of war from Elandslaagte. The men's first impression of the island was of complete desolation, but Governor Robert Sterndale and the island's residents went out of their way to treat the prisoners with dignity.

Two camps housed the prisoners: Deadwood, which had a beautiful view, and Broadbottom. The camps were on a plateau accessible via a shortcut known as Jacob's Ladder, a 699-step staircase. A commandant managed each camp. Initially, up to 12 men had to share a single tent in Deadwood, so the men were allowed to build their own shelters out of wood, canvas and zinc. This is how Blikkiesdorp (tin town) got its name, and how Lappiesdorp (cloth or rag town) came into being later at Broadbottom camp.

The British authorities decided to house Free Staters and Transvalers in separate camps to defuse the tension between the groups. An additional, small camp was built for Cape rebels. The 4th (Militia) Battalion of the Gloucestershire Regiment guarded the camps, relieved by the Royal Warwickshire Regiment. *Onversoenlikes* (recalcitrants) were held in Fort High Knoll. General Piet Cronjé lived with his wife in Kent Cottage, and General Ben Viljoen in Rose Cottage. Rev. JR Albertyn of the Wellington congregation came to St Helena voluntarily, and lived in Rose Bower.

Deadwood camp on St Helena. The prisoners later erected structures and businesses in the camp using whatever materials were available. This part of the camp was consequently known as Blikkiesdorp.

Prisoners of war who took the Oath of Neutrality while incarcerated were held separately. Their camp was called the 'Judas' camp and, also, the 'Jam' camp, as these prisoners were rewarded for their cooperation with an extra ration of jam.

The prisoners spent their days working with their hands between roll calls (which they referred to derisively as *rou kool*, Afrikaans for 'raw cabbage'). They also started businesses in the camp, such as the Presidentskafee (President's Café), which served pancakes and ginger beer. One Kootjie Doelemans, a Dutchman, even ran a bar (illegally, of course). Those who undertook not to try to escape were granted parole,

A chessboard made by Johannes Marte Mante, who was captured at Elandslaagte. The wood comes from a cedar tree near the erstwhile residence of Napoleon on St Helena. The chessboard shows watercolour scenes of St Helena sights, as well as Deadwood camp, Longwood House (where Napoleon lived during his exile) and Fort High Knoll.

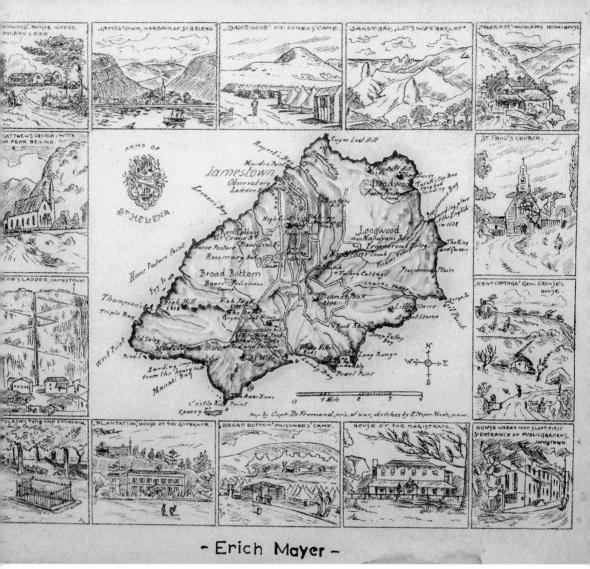

– Erich Mayer –

A watercolour sketch of St Helena by renowned artist Erich Mayer. Mayer drew this map during his incarceration on the island; it is framed by sketches of St Helena sights. Mayer was a surveyor who left Germany for South Africa in 1898, settling in the Orange Free State. He fought with the Boers, but was captured at Mafeking in May 1900 and sent to St Helena. He painted portraits of presidents Paul Kruger and MT Steyn while on the island, and documented everyday camp life.

periodically, to visit Jamestown, and some were even permitted to take jobs there.

The prisoners founded cultural societies that performed plays and recitals, and presented debate nights. A newspaper (*Kamp Kruimels*), sport committees and Christian associations also sprang up, as did a camp school.

When peace was concluded, many prisoners of war agonised over whether to take the Oath of Neutrality. Most did, in the end, and they were repatriated. Of the 179 prisoners of war who died on the island, Renier Meyer was the youngest, at 16, and Arnoldus Meiering the oldest, at 74.

Bermuda

The Bermuda archipelago, about 11 272 km from Cape Town in the North Atlantic, comprises seven main islands and 125 smaller ones. Vegetation is sparse and fresh water scarce.

Britain's tenure on the islands dates back to its naval presence there during the American War of Independence. The lieutenant governor of the islands agreed, in early 1901, to allow prisoner-of-war camps to be constructed on Hawkins, Hinson, Morgan's, Darrell, Tucker's, Burt, Port and St George's islands. Port Island would house hospital and administrative headquarters for the camps.

The first group of 4 619 prisoners arrived on the SS *Armenian* at the end of June 1901.

Most Cape rebels were sent to Bermuda; St George's Island, in particular, held a large number of these in its military prison. The rebels had limited privileges and were required to do forced labour.

Prisoners organised a number of societies, such as Christian, sport and cultural groups, on the different islands, and supported them keenly. The governor founded the Boer Recreation Society in July 1901, and even built two tennis courts.

Islanders who supported the Boer cause distributed goods such as tobacco, clothing and sports equipment among the prisoners. These goods came from organisations such as the Lend a Hand Society in the United States. As part of

A group of Cape rebels in convict uniforms in Bermuda. The clothes display the well-known 'hoenderspoor' (chicken spoor) symbol that identifies all British military equipment.

their contribution to improving the prisoners' circumstances, such organisations even sold in the US some of the curios that the Boers made in the camps. This channelled income to the prisoners, some of which was spent at businesses inside the camps selling pancakes, ginger beer and even ice cream.

Philanthropists supplied school supplies and erected a marquee that served as a library for the several youngsters held in the Bermuda camps. The school's youngest pupil was nine-year-old Piet Cronjé from Bethulie.

The regular postal service brought news from family and friends, even though letters were always censored.

Rev. JR Albertyn saw to the men's souls, as he had done on St Helena.

The Bermuda camps held many prisoners who had taken the Oath of Neutrality. These prisoners were transferred to Tucker's Island when tensions rose between them and the prisoners who had not taken the Oath. The Tucker's Island camp became known as 'hensopper camp' as a result.

At the end of the war, there were 150 *onversoenlikes* (recalcitrants) held on Hawkins Island. By August 1904, 12 remained; some never returned to South Africa. The Cape rebels remained in Bermuda until January 1903. On their return, they were held in the jail at Tokai in the Cape until they were granted amnesty in March 1903.

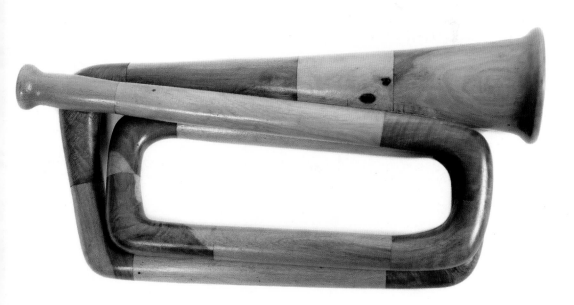

A cedarwood bugle made by 30-year-old Izaak Franz Ebersohn of the Kroonstad commando. He fashioned it using a pocket knife. 🔫

Ceylon

Britain sent 5 100 Boer prisoners of war to the island of Ceylon, which is now Sri Lanka. Diyatalawa camp, located about 300 km east of Colombo, the capital, was one of the largest prisoner-of-war camps to be established during the Anglo-Boer War. The need for it arose after General Marthinus Prinsloo and his men surrendered in the Brandwater Basin. Diyatalawa was built in July 1900.

The first group of prisoners of war arrived at the camp in August 1900. They lived in corrugated-iron structures, each of which had 65 beds. Barbed-wire fencing surrounded the camp, and it was brightly lit at night.

In time, additional smaller camps were built. Examples are the Ragama camp for troublemakers and Hambantota camp, which was a rest camp at the seaside for those who had taken the Oath of Neutrality. *Onversoenlikes* (recalcitrants) were detained in the Welikanda jail near Colombo.

Among the republican burghers in Ceylon were 49 Cape rebels, as well as prisoners from the Netherlands, Germany, United States, Ireland, France and Austria. There were even eight prisoners from Britain on the island. As in the camps in other locations, tensions built between Transvalers and Free Staters, so the camp was split in two. The Free Staters called their section Steynsburg, and the Transvalers christened theirs Krugersdorp.

The inmates passed the time by crafting souvenirs from ebony, satinwood and bone. They sold their handiwork to the camp guards and, later, to the local European population.

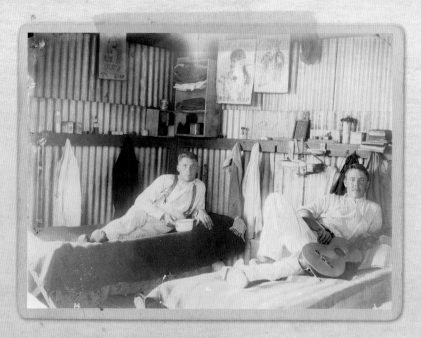

Two prisoners of war in their hut at Diyatalawa. Each hut's 65 residents chose a hut captain whose task it was, among others, to enforce camp rules.

Those prisoners of war on Ceylon, whom the British camp authorities viewed as 'trustworthy', were allowed to visit places of interest near their camp on Sundays.

A pith helmet of the type issued to prisoners of war on Ceylon. It was compulsory to wear these helmets when outdoors. Ordinary burghers had blue helmet bands, with red for officers, yellow for hut captains and black for rebels. This helmet belonged to 18-year-old Nicolas Philippus Landman of the Smithfield commando.

The more entrepreneurial among the prisoners soon had shops and cafés up and running, peddling sweet treats.

Sports and cultural activities were popular: the Boeren Muziek Gezelschap gave recitals, the Zastron Zang Koor and Wepener Zang Koor held singing evenings, and a newspaper called *De Prikkeldraad* reported on camp events. Six ministers counselled the camp's two congregations.

There were nearly 500 youths in the camp, who needed schooling and catechism classes. Adult prisoners who had not had the opportunity to complete their schooling in their own youth used the camp schools as an opportunity to broaden their education.

There were 21 escape attempts at Diyatalawa, despite the camp's heavy security. One of the best-known escapes involved the so-called five swimmers, a group of men who jumped off the SS *Catalonia* outside Colombo harbour on their way to Ceylon. They swam to the *Gherson*, a Russian ship, then took a protracted detour back to South Africa via Russia, Germany and the Netherlands.

By October 1902, about 4 372 of the Ceylon prisoners of war had taken the Oath of Neutrality, securing their return to South Africa. Some refused, and were still on the island a year later. Henry Engelbrecht of Bethulie was one of these: he died on the island in 1924, having never returned home.

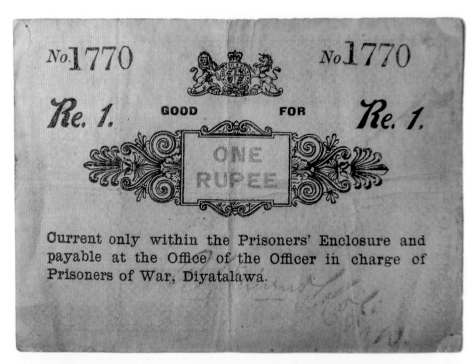

British camp authorities feared that the prisoners of war would use the money they earned to bribe the locals to help them escape. They decreed that all cash was to be handed over to the camp commandant, and later printed paper money that was only valid inside Diyatalawa. These 'good fors' were issued in 50-cent and one-, five- and ten-rupee denominations. 🔫

Brooches in the form of photo frames were handmade by Boer prisoners of war from material such as bone, horn and wood. These brooches were often sent to loved ones in the concentration camps.

India

The prisoner-of-war camps in India were widely scattered, from the foothills of the Himalayas and present-day Pakistan to the south coast. The first Indian camp was prepared in March 1901, inside the walls of an old fort at Ahmednagar.

A month later, the *Hawarden Castle* docked in Bombay (now Mumbai) with the first group of 512 prisoners of war. Shortly afterwards, the *Roslin Castle* arrived, carrying 507 men. The Indian camps would ultimately hold 9 551 men, of whom 139 died, mostly of dysentery.

Scores of diaries and letters testify to the fact that India was a culture shock for most of the Boers held there, but that the country, with its temples and foreign ways, fascinated them at the same time. The intensity of this cultural experience was matched only by the extreme weather, which ranged from wind storms that damaged camps like Ahmednagar to severe drought, uncommonly high summer temperatures and flooding in monsoon season.

Other camps were established at Abbottabad (Kakool), Bellary, Bhim Tal, Fort Govindgarh, Dagshai and Solon, Kaity Nilghiris, Murree Hills, Satara, Shahjahanpur, Umballa, Sialkot and Trichinopoly.

The Dagshai and Solon camps opened only a few months before the war ended. Abbottabad, in present-day Pakistan, was one of the biggest camps, holding about 1 500 prisoners of war under Gurkha guard. The camp at Fort Govindgarh (Amritsar) was known as 'die Hel' (Hell), its proximity to the Himalayas and their moderating effect on temperatures notwithstanding. Murree Hills (Upper Topa), also in present-day Pakistan, was the northernmost prisoner-of-war camp. Its remote location made the chances of surviving an escape so slim that it was the only camp to have neither fences nor guards.

The Sialkot camp's 560 prisoners endured temperatures of up to 46°C and torrential monsoon rains. Trichinopoly, in the south, lay in a region so barren that water was scarce. Its sandstorms and excessive heat reminded the prisoners, who lived in thatched-roof huts, of the Kalahari. This camp was also fenced and floodlit.

The prisoners in India resisted signing the Oath of Neutrality so vehemently that General Koos de la Rey had to be sent there to win them over. This delay resulted in the last prisoners leaving the camp only in January 1904.

Boer prisoners of war in Hut 4 at Ahmednagar camp. The 1 200 prisoners lived in 19 large buildings within the walls of Fort Govindargh. After the signing of the Peace of Vereeniging, all *onversoenlikes* (recalcitrants) in the Indian camps were sent to Ahmednagar. It was the last camp in India to close, in January 1904.

A photo frame made of 980 pieces of Indian cedarwood. Antonie
Philippus de Waal, a 42-year-old from Pretoria, made it while incarcerated
at the Shahjahanpur camp. It took four men eight days to cut the pieces,
and De Waal three days to affix them – without any glue or nails.

John de Villiers' Escape

John Louw de Villiers was 29 when he went on commando in 1899. After fighting in the battles of Talana and Modderspruit and participating in the Siege of Ladysmith, he was captured near Pietersburg in April 1901.

He was initially detained at Pretoria's so-called Rest Camp and at Tin Town in Ladysmith. In May, he was sent to India with 500 other prisoners of war and eight officers on a ship that docked at Madras (now Chennai). His final destination was the newly opened Trichinopoly camp.

Camp life did not suit De Villiers at all. Within six months, he had an escape plan: he would disguise himself as an Indian and simply walk out the gate. He did just that on 10 March 1902, clad in Indian dress, alongside a goods cart. He travelled to Pondicherry, then under French control, by rail and on foot; he then boarded a Norwegian ship to Marseille and returned, ultimately, to South Africa.

De Villiers wrote about his exploits in the 1903 book *Hoe ik ontsnapte: verhaal van een merkwaardige ontsnapping van een Boer uit Engelsch-India* (How I escaped: The story of a Boer's remarkable escape from British India). An extract follows:

Everything was placed in readiness in Mr M's room for me to complete my transformation later that afternoon. Razor, shaving brush, 15 to 20 blackened corks, everything was gathered for me, immediately after signing the attendance register, to complete my disguise ... when I entered the room my friend M shaved off my beard and trimmed my black moustache short ... Mr W blackened my hands, and then my arms and, when I was shaven, my face ...

But when I looked in the mirror my lips were too red and my eyes too white. An inkpot stood on the table; I stuck my finger into the ink and smeared it on my lips and over my eyes. Although it hurt, it had the desired effect. My lips now had a bluish colour and my eyes were no longer noticeable. When I walked past the last hut and came within sight of the gate I met the censor ... who barely took notice of me. Everything was going well.

The cart, on its daily route from the shop to the gate, had almost reached the gate and I was obliged to run a little way to draw level with it at the gate ... when I reached the cart I had to be careful to remain unseen. I therefore stood behind the wheels so that he driver could not see me ... when the gate opened, the cart passed through it and I took hold of the canopy as if I belonged there ... in this way, I walked through the main gate.

The cart turned off to the left past the guardhouse. I followed the road to Trichinopoly, straight through the huts of the English troops.

John de Villiers

In February 1902, John de Villiers ordered three sets of clothes from Madras – the same clothes as worn by the Indians who worked as servants in the camps. He gave two sets to the servants and used the third to disguise himself. The turban and cricket shoes were also part of his outfit.

Passing the Time

For many Boer prisoners of war, finding things to do to pass the time in the overseas camps was a challenge. Many, especially the younger ones, played sport: tennis, cricket, football, rugby, athletics, boxing, fencing, and Boeresports such as jukskei were popular, and different camps or clubs sometimes staged competitions.

Others kept themselves busy by making curios with pocket knives, saws and, later, windmill-powered lathes. Some made their own tools, such as drills and chisels. Curios were made from whatever materials were available: bone, wood, rock, even metal. Walking sticks, boxes, photo frames, pipes, carts, rings, brooches, paper cutters, serviette rings and watch chains were particularly popular, and were sold not only within the camps but also by foreign organisations on the prisoners' behalf.

It goes without saying that socialising was important to the Boers. The societies they founded – including debating, singing, music and drama societies – helped to relieve the monotony of camp life. The debating society was especially popular, as it gave expression to the prisoners' patriotism.

Some prisoners presented concerts using instruments that were brought in or made, featuring mostly Dutch or English songs, as Afrikaans was still in its infancy. Others developed their creative talents by writing poems or essays. National days and folk festivals were also celebrated.

Camp photographers had studios that the prisoners of war visited frequently for individual portraits and group photographs with their tent mates. Photographs of the camp itself were also taken.

Many camps had coffee houses and cafés where the prisoners of war could talk to their hearts' content and, if only for a moment, forget about the reality of their situation over a pancake or other sweet treat.

Camp newspapers kept everyone apprised of the latest camp activities. They also contained advertisements, reports about the societies' projects, and extracts from the Scriptures.

The programme for a boxing tournament held on Saturday 19 July 1902 in the Diyatalawa recreation hall – two months after the Peace of Vereeniging.

One E Nash presented this cricket bat to 27-year-old prisoner of war Charles William Morgan of Bloemfontein in September 1901 after a match between the Ahmednagar Boer Cricket Club and the Royal Field Artillery. Morgan scored 77 runs for the Ahmednagar Boer Cricket Club.

The Amritsar Cricket Club on the stairs of one of the bastions at Fort Govindgarh. Prisoners of war played all kinds of sports within the walls of the fort.

Youngsters in the Camps

by Dané Swanepoel

The two Boer republics viewed boys as adults at the age of 16 – old enough to be commandeered for military service. Even younger boys went on commando, in some cases. These youngsters were known as *penkoppe* (see page 226).

British forces did not discriminate when they captured *penkoppe* in the field, sending them with the adult commando members to prisoner-of-war camps. British forces feared the potential for young boys to join Boer forces as *penkoppe*. When they went to remove women and children from Boer farms, then, they would take boys as young as nine as a preventive measure; even boys as young as six were sent to the camps.

The prisoner-of-war camps held a total of 1 389 boys between the ages of six and 15. Camp authorities ensured that the boys were schooled by prisoners of war with backgrounds in education. Older prisoners of war also gave catechism classes.

The boys gave the British soldiers hell with their pranks. They were especially fond of political offences, such as singing the anthems of their republics. British soldiers threatened corporal punishment, to no avail. In one case, a group of youngsters had to plant trees as hard labour. They spent the whole day digging the holes, then planted the trees late in the afternoon before hurrying back to camp. When the officer went to inspect their work the next day, he found that they had deliberately planted all the trees upside down!

A group of boys in the Green Point camp, before being sent to a prisoner-of-war camp overseas.

A toy baboon made in Bermuda by 30-year-old Cornelis Johannes Human of Jacobsdal.

This pouch, containing 19 marbles, belonged to a boy who was held in the Green Point camp.

Where does the name 'penkop' come from?

There are two theories about the origin of the name 'penkop'. The first holds that it refers to the way in which young boys' hair used to be cut – close to the skull, so that it stood up like little quills. According to the second theory, the name equates the boys with young blue wildebeest bulls, whose underdeveloped horns – 'pennetjies' – are straight, and have not yet developed the sweeping curve of those of the older bulls.

Nine-year-old Petrus Willem (Piet) Cronjé of the farm Klein Vischat, outside Bethulie, and 11-year-old Tjaart van der Walt play marbles in the Hinson prisoner-of-war camp in Bermuda. The boys were the youngest prisoners of war on the islands; Piet was captured on his parents' farm.

A cedarwood photo frame made by JP Eksteen, showing a mother at prayer. The photograph shows nine-year-old Petrus Willem (Piet) Cronjé (also in the photo above) and his brother Schalk Jacobus Cronjé. The Cronjé family was detained in the Springfontein concentration camp. The two boys were reunited with their family on their repatriation in September 1902.

Prisoners of war in Diyatalawa camp, in Ceylon, with
some of the tiepins and brooches (see below) they
made by hand from bone, using coping saws and files.

Interned in Portugal

In 1900, the tide of the war began to turn against the Boer republics. A number of republican sympathisers in the Cape Colony and Natal, along with a few Cape rebels, took their families and retreated northwards. When Bloemfontein fell, a few Free State families joined them. This 150-strong band of refugees fled to the Transvaal.

A few months after the fall of Pretoria, they crossed into Portuguese East Africa (now Mozambique) under General FJ Pienaar's leadership. International practice meant that Portugal had to intern the group until the end of the war. The group had by that time grown to about 1 019, 178 of whom were women and children. The colonial authorities could not accommodate such a large group adequately, so they sent the refugees on to Portugal. Pressure from the British government also had a hand in this decision: the British saw the group, potentially just one border crossing away from re-entering the war, as a threat.

It took about five months for the first group of 691 internees to leave for Portugal, in February 1901. The rest of the group followed shortly afterwards. They were housed in six different locations, each with its own Portuguese military commander. One of these was the Convent of the Order of Christ (Convento da Ordem

An urn, known as the 'Bilha Boer', or Boer Urn, made in 1900 by the Portuguese artist Avelino António Soares Belo. The original was given to President Paul Kruger, and five replicas were made. The coats of arms of the two republics appear on the urn, as does the figure of a triumphant Boer fighter crushing British forces. One of the internees was a model for the Boer figure. 🔫

de Christo), outside the little town of Tomar. General Pienaar, who was granted an audience with King Carlos I of Portugal in May 1901, was lodged here with his family and a few others.

The internees were divided into three larger groups of over 300. One group was sent to Alcobaça, 108 km north of Lisbon, where they were lodged in the Real Abadia de Santa Maria de Alcobaça. Another group of 340 went to the coastal town of Peniche, where they were accommodated in a fort. (This group included 83 members of the Transvaal police and 20 members of the State Artillery.) The third group was sent to Caldas da Rainha. Portugal may have been one of Britain's oldest allies, but its people were sympathetic to the internees, giving them wide-ranging freedom of movement.

Of those interned in Portugal, eight died at sea. Illness claimed another 17 in Portugal. The oldest was 58-year-old Christiaan Jacobus van der Walt of Johannesburg; the youngest was Doris Maria d'Azinhoes Vorster, barely two months old.

Alcobaça was renowned for its pottery. A staunch supporter of the Boers, Lieutenant AAC da Costa, ordered a hand-painted plate like this one to be made and given to each family interned at Alcobaça. This plate belonged to Johannes Jurie Human Claase of Barkly West.

When peace was concluded, most of the internees took the Oath of Neutrality and made their way home aboard the SS *Bavarian* in July 1902.

Children of internees at the Boer school in Caldas da Rainha. Also pictured are their teachers, J de Bruijn (at front) and JDM Swart (at rear left), and principal RA den Ouden.

The Undesirables: Port Alfred and Matjiesfontein

Many in the Cape Colony strongly opposed Britain's military action against the civilian population during the war's guerrilla phase, and the concentration camp system invoked the ire of Cape Colony Afrikaners.

Criticism came from quarters such as Rev. Johan George Steytler of the Theological Seminary in Stellenbosch, and from teachers and ordinary citizens. The British military authorities endeavoured to identify these detractors and

A group of undesirables.

A telegram to Johanna Vosloo of Somerset East, ordering her to report to the local magistrate. She was informed shortly afterwards that she would be sent to Port Alfred. Vosloo had started a school for Afrikaans-speaking children in Somerset East; the school was closed and she was sent away. ✎

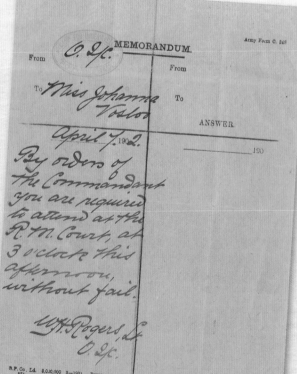

invoke its powers under martial law to remove them from society. They were to be exiled to places where their pronouncements would have the least possible impact. These *ongewenstes*, or undesirables, were detained without trial, in many cases, for the duration of the war.

Undesirables from the Cradock, Graaff-Reinet, Somerset East, Bedford and Aberdeen districts, for example, were interned at Port Alfred or Matjiesfontein. Generally, undesirables had to carry their own costs of travelling to the internment camps, and their families were responsible for their upkeep there.

Undesirables who were sent to Matjiesfontein had to pay five shillings a month for a tent that housed up to eight others. Their food cost an additional two shillings a day. This sort of treatment by the British military in the Cape Colony led to great dissatisfaction with the colonial government.

Walking sticks made by undesirables interned at Port Alfred. Each walking stick contains inscriptions and names of the maker's fellow undesirables. One such inscription reads 'Alleen verbannen van Cradock naar Port Alfred, 20.7.1901' (Exiled from Cradock to Port Alfred, 20 July 1901).

General Christiaan de Wet (in the middle with pointing finger) conveys the news of the peace treaty and its terms to residents of the Norvalspont concentration camp in the southern Orange Free State.

CHAPTER 10

Peace and the Post-war Years

The Peace Negotiations

The first recognised peace negotiations, between Lord Kitchener and General Louis Botha, began at Middelburg in February 1901. President MT Steyn strongly opposed any agreement that failed to recognise the two republics as independent states, however. When the parties could not reach consensus, the Middelburg talks broke up.

By early 1902, even the Bittereinders were starting to realise that the war was unsustainable. The devastating effects of the scorched-earth policy and the suffering in the concentration camps created deep concern. No less of a concern was the increasing number of armed black fighters who had rallied on the side of the British, and the white turncoats who had taken up arms against their own.

The Dutch government had offered to mediate, an offer that the British government dismissed out of hand. This did, however, lead to renewed peace negotiations using the Middelburg proposals as a point of departure.

In April, representatives of the two republican governments met at Klerksdorp to discuss the transfer of power. They then entered into discussions about a peace settlement with Kitchener in Pretoria. The republics' request for the burghers in the field to be consulted was granted.

The commandos then appointed representatives who engaged with delegates of the two republics between 15 and 31 May in Vereeniging. Topics discussed there included the republics' situation from a military standpoint, and the conditions under which the republics would consider

Acting Transvaal president Schalk Burger addresses residents of the Merebank concentration camp in June 1902 after peace was declared.

ABOVE Melrose House, which Lord Roberts and, later, Lord Kitchener used as their headquarters in Pretoria. The peace treaty that became known as the Peace of Vereeniging was also signed here.

BELOW The pen used by Lord Kitchener to sign the Peace of Vereeniging on 31 May 1902.

relinquishing power. Many still hoped that the republics could retain their independence, one way or another.

A subcommittee comprising Generals JBM Hertzog and Jan Smuts (both legal experts) and Lords Milner and Kitchener settled on a draft peace treaty after debating each of the draft clauses extensively. Boer republican independence was not an option for the British government. The latter approved a proposal in London, presenting it to the representatives assembled at Vereeniging as its final offer.

President MT Steyn stepped down due to ill health on 29 May, and General Christiaan de Wet was appointed acting state president.

The peace terms were put to a vote at 2 pm on 31 May. There were 54 votes for, and six against. Jozua François Naudé, father of the well-known Rev. Beyers Naudé, was among those who opposed the settlement. According to *Die Bittereinde Vrede*, acting Transvaal president Schalk Burger declared during the vote: 'We stand, here, at the grave of the two Republics.'

At 11.05 pm that night, the Peace of Vereeniging was signed at Melrose House in Pretoria by a small group of Boer delegates. Hand outstretched, Lord Kitchener then declared, 'we are all good friends now'.

The agreement signalled the end of the republics' independence, but also heralded a new era in South African history and politics.

The Costs of the War

During its planning, the War Office in London projected that the war against the Boer republics, whose forces were an estimated 50 000 to 56 000 strong, would require 75 000 soldiers. It would also, according to the War Office, be over within months.

Not only did the war last for close on three years, but 448 000 British and imperial soldiers would be required to fight it. The Treasury budgeted £10 million for a war that cost £217 million in the end. The British public was largely unaware of the war's true cost – until, that is, press photographs of dozens of dead British soldiers on the battlefield at Spioenkop brought home the gruesome reality.

Despite the best efforts to keep an accurate count of British deaths, it was not always possible. Sources differ, therefore, but the casualty figure on the British side – the so-called butcher's bill – is thought to stand at 97 477 men. Of these, 20 870 died in battle or of sickness.

Some of the severely wounded died later in Britain, which may account for the differences between the figures cited by British sources. On top of this, the war took the lives of 400 346 horses, donkeys and mules.

About 6 594 Boer fighters died, a figure that includes about 778 prisoner-of-war deaths in the camps and at sea. For the Boers, however, the highest death toll was not among combatants on the battlefield but among women and children in the concentration camps.

A state funeral – in Pretoria and many rural towns – for those who died in the Battle of Elandslaagte on 21 October 1899 made a very clear impression of the impact of the war on the citizens of the two republics. As the war progressed, Boer casualties became increasingly common. Burghers continued to aim to give their dead a dignified burial, however.

The Guild of Loyal Women came into being in South Africa during the war. This association of English-speaking women tended British graves during and after the war – until 1910, when the Union government became responsible for doing so. (In 2010, the Commonwealth War Graves Commission, in partnership with the South African Heritage Resources Agency, launched a project to repair the graves of all imperial soldiers who perished during the Anglo-Boer War. The project is financed by the Commonwealth War Graves Commission.)

Burghers are reinterred at Heidelberg shortly after the war. Note the pulpit and gallery draped in crêpe.

Shortly after the war, uniform cast-iron crosses were placed on the graves of British soldiers. Each cross was individually cast and shows the soldier's regiment, service number, date of death, initials and surname.

Returning and Rebuilding

'The country was as waste as the edge of the Sahara; about the only cattle we saw were carcasses rotting on the wayside; we passed only one farmhouse that was intact; we stopped at two villages, about one-fifth of one being destroyed, and of the other not a single roof remained.'

These were the impressions of British politician and future prime minister Ramsay MacDonald during a 1902 visit to towns such as Lindley, Vrede, Bethlehem, Reitz and Senekal. Peace had been concluded in May of that year, and there was nothing left for the Bittereinders, the women and children from the concentration camps, and the prisoners of war to do but return to the wasteland that was the Orange Free State and Transvaal.

The war impoverished thousands of Afrikaners; they returned from the war to little more than significant economic, political and social challenges. Workers' colonies, such as Kransdraai at Bethulie and Mushroom Valley at Winburg, took up some destitute families, who worked for the new colonial government for little pay on dam-building projects, among others.

The trauma of families who had lost loved ones in the conflict was still raw. Long-separated husbands and wives had become strangers; widows struggled to get by on their own; multitudes of orphans cried out for care in newly established orphanages. The rift between Bittereinders and joiners remained so wide that it even seeped into church communities. At every turn, the Afrikaners were confronted with the English language, which had become the new medium of instruction in schools and was in exclusive use in the courts and other state departments.

Black South Africans were also disenchanted. The British government's promises of political rights had come to nothing, and black people who had established themselves on white farmers' land during the war were informed that pre-war property rights would be upheld.

Life for the former republicans did, however, start to settle. British forces trickled home, until only a few garrisons remained; war materiel was auctioned off; hard work rebuilt the farms. More than ever before, Afrikaners nurtured their language and culture. As a counterweight to the anglicisation of schools, Christian National Education schools were founded, which furthered Afrikaans language and culture.

In 1905, Sir Henry Campbell-Bannerman's Liberal government took office in Britain. The new ministry was well-disposed to the Afrikaners, and Lord Milner was replaced as high commissioner for southern Africa. Soon, the Transvaal and Orange River Colonies were granted self-rule. Afrikaners began to remobilise politically through General Louis Botha's Het Volk party in the Transvaal and General JBM Hertzog's Orangia Unie in the former Orange Free State, which took the reins of self-rule with great zeal.

The Neser family in 1907 at the grave of one of the children who died in a concentration camp.

Staffordshire spaniels came in sets of two and were usually
displayed on the mantelpiece. On returning to their
decimated farm, the Scholtz family of Dewetsdorp found
this lone figurine, the sole surviving item in the ruins.

ABOVE Wheat from a store that was burnt down on the farm Broekpoort in the Smithfield district.

BELOW After the war Jan Gildenhuis and his family returned to a burnt-down farmhouse on Hoenderkop farm in the Winburg district.

'When we approached the farmhouse, I saw tears running down my dear father's cheeks. My mother turned her face so we couldn't see … Of course there was no trace of our furniture, and the house was completely empty … Everything had grown wild … almost all the big trees were dead … The water ditches were all overgrown and wild animals had moved into the house … I could see the look of helplessness on the faces of my father and mother … everything they'd sweated and worked for was destroyed and gone.'
– Sarah Raal in *The Lady Who Fought*

Jan Adriaan Grobbelaar's farm, Groot Marsfontein, in the Bethulie district, before and after the war.

B.O. 1581. A6468/3.

1666 Government of the Orange River Colony.

C.J.C. No....................

LEDGER FOLIO...365...

REPATRIATION RECOVERIES BRANCH,
TREASURY, O.R.C.

1ˢᵗ October 1905.

Received from J C Pretorius

Strangers Rest Senekal

through the Central Judicial Commission the Sum of £25

Twenty five pounds shillings pence awarded to him from the £3,000,000 granted under the Terms of Surrender and now placed to the credit of his account in the books of this Department.

W. Stopmaff

Accountant.

A receipt for compensation money paid to JC Pretorius of Senekal. Only a small part of the amount claimed was generally paid out – if the claim was honoured at all.

The Delegation to Europe

At Vereeniging, the decision was made to send Generals Louis Botha, Christiaan de Wet and Koos de la Rey to Europe to raise funds, specifically for widows and orphans. The delegates also hoped that they could negotiate directly with the British government about concessions to certain clauses in the peace treaty.

The generals received a hero's welcome in Cape Town, where spirited crowds followed them wherever they went. The party that set sail aboard the RMS *Saxon* on 30 July 1902 included another three generals, Rev. JD Kestell, Koos de la Rey's wife, Nonnie, and Botha's wife, Annie. At sea, Kestell helped General De Wet to write his memoirs.

The generals were all too aware that they would need to handle the British government and media with great diplomacy if they wanted to win the treaty concessions they so desired. Even before docking at Southampton, however, they were placed in a thorny situation; they received an invitation to attend a review of the Royal Navy in honour of the coronation of King Edward VII (Queen Victoria had died in January 1901). The invitation was declined, but during the review they did pay a courtesy visit to Joseph Chamberlain, Lord Roberts and Lord Kitchener – aboard a warship at anchor in Southampton harbour. Emily Hobhouse visited the Boer party aboard the *Saxon* too.

Large crowds awaited them on British soil, especially at London's Waterloo station on the day of the delegation's visit to sympathisers such as David Lloyd George, Ramsay MacDonald and WT Stead. Shortly before they left for the Netherlands, the King received them warmly.

Their reception in Rotterdam was even heartier, however. Dr Willem Leyds – former state secretary of the South African Republic and special envoy in

Generals Christiaan de Wet, Koos de la Rey and Louis Botha during their visit to Europe.

The three generals on the balcony of their hotel shortly after arriving in the Netherlands.

Brussels – and other officials from the former republics' foreign missions joined the delegation, which paid its respects to Paul Kruger and MT Steyn. The latter was in the Netherlands for medical treatment.

While the delegation was in Brussels, the generals were given a date for a meeting with British colonial secretary Joseph Chamberlain. On the agenda for this 5 September meeting was amnesty for the Cape and Natal rebels, increased compensation for the former burghers of the two republics, and the return to South Africa, from Europe, of the former republican bureaucracy.

The success of the talks would prove limited, however: compensation was not increased and, while the rebels were granted amnesty in the long run, it was conditional. Regarding the bureaucracy, those who had been involved in the former republics' European missions were, indeed,

allowed to return home, but only if they took the Oath of Neutrality.

The generals returned to Europe and visited Germany, but were not granted an audience with Kaiser Wilhelm II.

Before their homeward journey commenced, on 13 December, the generals visited London again for old times' sake. Here, Botha attended a House of Commons debate about the Boers' compensation claim, and the delegation paid King Edward VII a final courtesy visit at Buckingham Palace. When the king offered them each a knighthood, they declined.

The generals did not raise as much money as they had hoped to, but they did make valuable contacts – especially with British politicians such as Lloyd George and MacDonald. After the 1906 general election, these contacts would stand them in good stead.

This sword of honour was presented to General Christiaan de Wet during the generals' visit to Germany.

Hobhouse's Spinning and Weaving Schools

by Dané Swanepoel

When Emily Hobhouse returned to South Africa in 1903, she experienced the former republics' post-war poverty and misery first hand. She recalled her visits to the concentration camps, and the Boer women's creativity and efficiency in needlework. She resolved to start home industries to help Boer women back onto their feet.

Initially, she wanted to teach the women the art of lace-making. To familiarise herself with the process, she started by visiting lace shops in London. Her research also took her to Venice and Brussels.

Back in England, she sought the advice of one Mrs JR Green, a home industry expert, about lace-making. To Hobhouse's astonishment, Green regarded lace-making as an impractical way for home industries to earn an income, and was far more interested in spinning and weaving.

Emily Hobhouse (circled) with Constance Cloete and Hester Marais on the stoep of the Philippolis weaving school in 1905. Two housekeepers, Johanna and Marie, accompany them.

A lace collar with a buffalo thorn (*Wag-'n-bietjiebos*) motif, made at the lace-making school in Koppies.

Hobhouse knew that wool was readily available in South Africa. It would be more practical, she realised, to open spinning and weaving schools where women could learn to make blankets, carpets and textiles. The ordinary citizen would find lace expensive, but commodities made of wool would find a ready market in South Africa.

Financing the schools was one of Hobhouse's biggest challenges, however. She approached the Women and Children Distress Fund and presented her suggestions. The fund was renamed the Boer Home Industries and Aid Society, and enough money was raised to fund the project for a year. The first spinning and weaving school opened in Philippolis on 15 March 1905. By 1908, both the former republics had their own schools, and basket-making and leatherwork had also started taking root.

A spinning wheel that Emily Hobhouse brought to South Africa.

Hobhouse did not give up on her dream to open a lace-making school, however. With Johanna Rood, she left for Italy 1908, where the two studied the art. The following year, she established a lace-making school in Koppies, in the northern Free State. Its first student was Miss H Kriel. Koppies was small, however, and its residents were poor, so the school struggled to attract enrolments. Home circles were formed as a result.

The fact that all the materials that lace-making required had to be imported made the lace expensive to produce, but those who could afford to support the school did so.

The spinning and weaving industries experienced a revival in the 1930s. The lace-making school, however, was closed in 1938; its outlays had simply become too great.

Lest We Forget ...

The idea of a monument to the wartime suffering of Boer women and children originated with President MT Steyn. At the end of the war, a Monuments Commission was established to raise the funds required to bring this idea to life.

The design put forward by Pretoria architect Frans Soff and sculptor Anton van Wouw was accepted with few amendments. Van Wouw chose the location for the monument, and the Bloemfontein city council donated the land. While the Kroonstad-sandstone outer wall and obelisk were taking shape, Van Wouw went to Italy to sculpt the central figures and two side panels. These would depict aspects of concentration-camp life.

Emily Hobhouse was in Rome at the time, and visited Van Wouw in his Canova studio. She found his work unimpressive, and suggested that he visit the Vatican and view Michelangelo's *Pietà* for inspiration. There is evidence of him having done so in his final design.

During one of Hobhouse's subsequent visits to Van Wouw, she described to him a scene that she had witnessed at Springfontein station during the war. A group of women and children had just arrived – in the rain, in open-topped carriages. While they were waiting at the station to be transported to the already-overcrowded Springfontein concentration camp, Hobhouse watched as a child died in his mother's arms. She described to Van Wouw the profound heartache that she had seen on the mother's face. Her moving description would be the ultimate inspiration for Van Wouw's sculpture.

Rachel (Tibbie) Steyn, wife of former president Steyn, unveiled the central group on Hobhouse's behalf at the National Women's Monument on 16 December 1913 (Hobhouse was too ill to travel further than Beaufort West). In his speech,

former president Steyn said: 'This monument is not here to torture anyone, or to level eternal blame, but is placed here out of pure piety.'

A large crowd attended the unveiling, including Boer generals such as Christiaan de Wet and Louis Botha (prime minister of the Union of South Africa at the time). De Wet delivered an inflammatory speech that threatened to deepen the political rift in Afrikaner ranks.

Botha was not in favour of the monument, fearing that it would open old wounds between English and Afrikaans speakers. However, the monument was not erected for political reasons.

Four prominent Afrikaners were buried at the monument as the years passed: Steyn (1916), De Wet (1922), Rev. JD Kestell (1941) and Tibbie Steyn (1955). Emily Hobhouse herself was laid to rest there in 1926.

Tibbie Steyn unveiled the Women's Monument on 16 December 1913 on Emily Hobhouse's behalf.

Anton van Wouw's original design for the central group of
figures left Emily Hobhouse decidedly unimpressed.

The 1914 Rebellion

When the First World War broke out, in 1914, it was unthinkable, for many Afrikaners, that Louis Botha, by then prime minister of the Union of South Africa, should take sides with Britain. After all the support that the German public and press had given the two republics during the Anglo-Boer War, there was widespread resentment that the British government had asked Botha to invade German South West Africa (now Namibia).

Prominent Afrikaners – former president MT Steyn, Generals Christiaan de Wet and Koos de la Rey, and high-ranking officers of the Union Defence Force such as General Christiaan Beyers, Lieutenant Colonel Manie Maritz and Major Jan Kemp – spoke out against the request

The car in which General Koos de la Rey was fatally shot in September 1914. His driver tried to run a police roadblock, intended for the Foster gang, in Johannesburg.

and advocated neutrality instead. They also saw the outbreak of war in Europe as a chance of winning the republics' independence back from Britain.

Tensions ran high after De la Rey was shot dead by accident at a police roadblock in Langlaagte, Johannesburg, on 15 September 1914. The roadblock had been erected in an effort to catch the notorious Foster gang.

Simmering dissatisfaction boiled over into an armed rebellion when Maritz, commander of the military camp at Upington, joined German forces in South West Africa on 10 October.

Rebel commandos soon materialised in the Transvaal and Orange Free State. About 7 000 men mobilised in the Free State (where De Wet took the lead), 3 000 in the Transvaal and 2 000 in the Cape. The government responded by declaring martial law on 12 October.

A month later, the Union Defence Force defeated De Wet's commando south of Winburg and captured De Wet two weeks later.

On 16 November, General Christiaan Beyers' commando fell near Bultfontein. In a bid to evade capture, Beyers drowned, on 8 December, while trying to cross the Vaal River.

Commandant Jopie Fourie made the grave mistake of joining the rebels before resigning from the Active Citizen Force. Forced to hand himself over on 16 December, he was found guilty of high treason and executed by firing squad in Pretoria. On 2 February 1915, Kemp and his men, as well as Maritz's men, surrendered in the northwestern Cape Province.

Thus ended the rebellion, which had claimed the lives of about 190 rebels and 132 government troops. Only 281 rebels appeared in court. The guilty were sentenced to a maximum jail term of seven years and a fine of up to £2 000. Widespread sympathy for the rebels' cause meant that all of them were released from prison before the end of 1916.

The 1914 Rebellion may have been short-lived, but it left an indelible mark on South African politics. Botha's South African Party lost a great deal of support to the newly established National Party under General JBM Hertzog.

The Bloemfontein jail, where General Christiaan de Wet and other rebels were held before being transferred to the Johannesburg Fort.

A tray of cotton reels that General Christiaan de Wet made for his daughter-in-law, Cornelia de Wet, while in detention in the Johannesburg Fort.

The Dekoratie voor Trouwe Dienst and Die Lint voor Wonden

Unlike their uniformed British counterparts, who were honoured with medals and decorations for their service during the Anglo-Boer War, burghers and officers who had fought for the two republics went unrewarded. This was a source of dissatisfaction for former Boer officers who went on to join the Union Defence Force.

Efforts to rectify this gathered pace after the First World War. In 1920, a War Medal for all burghers who had fought in the war was approved. The Dekoratie voor Trouwe Dienst (Decoration for Loyal Service) was also approved for officers, as was Die Lint voor Wonden (Ribbon for the Wounded) for those who had been wounded in the war. The War Medal would be issued with a certificate to those who qualified.

Prospective recipients were required to apply in writing to the adjutant general of the Union Defence Force. Wherever possible, the burgher's former commanding officer would need to verify the application, and a short record of service would need to accompany it.

The medals were politicised, however, for being an initiative of General Jan Smuts's South African Party. General JBM Hertzog and his National Party levelled heavy criticism at Smuts for siding with Britain in the First World War, and dismissed the medals as a British tradition that had no place in South Africa. Many Afrikaners chose not to apply. Of the 14 594 applications received, 13 751 War Medals were awarded.

Only 591 officers received the Dekoratie voor Trouwe Dienst, with the last one awarded on 25 July 1944 to Commandant Josephus Janse van Rensburg of the Brandfort commando. The equivalent of Britain's Distinguished Service Order (DSO), this decoration was not awarded to officers who had handed themselves over or taken the Oath of Neutrality before 31 May 1902. Other recipients included Red Cross staff, officers of the foreign corps, the chief war commissioner and assistant chief commissioner, the chief heliographist and the postmaster general.

The coat of arms of the Republic of the Orange Free State appears on one side of both the War Medal and the Dekoratie voor Trouwe Dienst, and that of the South African Republic on the reverse. The ribbon combines the colours of both republics' flags. A Free State burgher, then, would wear his medal or decoration with the Free State coat of arms facing outwards and the ribbon's white and orange bands on the left; a Transvaal burgher would face the Transvaal coat of arms outwards and the wear the ribbon's red and green bands on the left.

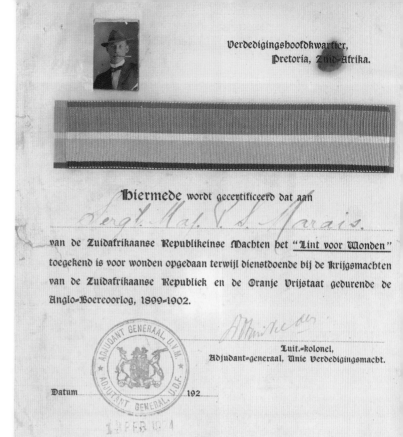

The Lint voor Wonden awarded to Paulus Stephanus Marais, who belonged to one of the Free State commandos. A photo of Marais was also attached to the certificate.

Certificate text:

Verdedigingshoofdkwartier,
Pretoria, Zuid-Afrika.

Hiermede wordt gecertificeerd dat aan

Serg. Maj. P.S. Marais.

van de Zuidafrikaanse Republikeinse Machten het "Lint voor Wonden" toegekend is voor wonden opgedaan terwijl dienstdoende bij de krijgsmachten van de Zuidafrikaanse Republiek en de Oranje Vrijstaat gedurende de Anglo-Boereoorlog, 1899-1902.

Luit.-kolonel,
Adjudant-generaal, Unie Verdedigingsmacht.

Datum _____ 192_

This medal group, which includes the Dekoratie voor Trouwe Dienst (far left) and the War Medal (second from left), was awarded to John Alexander Charles van Heerden after the war. Van Heerden was a field cornet in the Jacobsdal commando and later joined the Union Defence Force. The order of the colours on the ribbon of the Dekoratie voor Trouwe Dienst show that he was a burgher of the Orange Free State. However, for the purposes of this photo the medal was turned around to show the Transvaal coat of arms.

The War, 100 Years On

In the years immediately following the Anglo-Boer War, a surge of monuments, books and publications arose in its commemoration. Its centenary, from 1999 to 2002, evoked renewed interest in the war, which remains the largest military conflict ever to have played out on South African soil.

In the recent past, the War Museum of the Boer Republics embarked on three ambitious heritage projects that aim to interpret the war from the perspective of the present. The projects include the Heritage Quilt (2010), the Heritage Art Collection Project (2013) and the Garden of Remembrance (2015).

In 2010, the War Museum commissioned Naomi Moolman to craft a 6,38´ 3,34-m quilt depicting women and children's experiences before, during and after the war. It displays relatively unknown photographs, and is one of the museum's most popular attractions.

During the National Women's Monument centenary celebrations in 2013, the War Musuem approached 70 South African artists to create artworks depicting the universal suffering so keenly felt during the Anglo-Boer War.

Through this project, the museum sought to expand its existing art collection, which already contained pieces by renowned artists such as Anton van Wouw, Erich Mayer, Frans Oerder, Johannes Meintjes, WH Coetzer and many others. The art collection project inspired a new generation of artists to share their perspectives on the war; 130 new artworks were ultimately donated.

The War Museum unveiled its Garden of Remembrance in 2015. The garden contains the names of over 36 000 white and black women

One of many concentration camp rules was that all candles had to be extinguished at a specific time. Many mothers told of the agony of keeping vigil, in the dark, over their dying children to evade punishment. The title of the work by Jaco van Schalkwyk on the opposite page is *Sy het nie 'n kers gehad nie* (She had no candle, oil on canvas, 2013).

and children who died during the war, mainly in the concentration camps. A map in the garden also shows the locations of all the concentration camps that held black and white South Africans during the war.

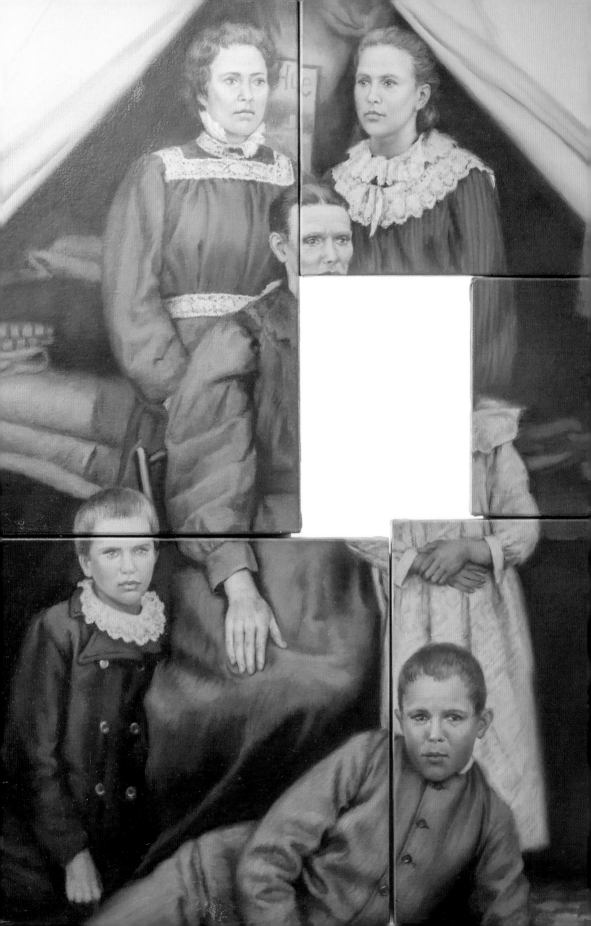

Bibliography

Amery, L.S. 1900–1906. *Times History of the War in South Africa 1899–1902, Vol. I–IV.* London: S. Low, Marston & Co.

Barnard, S.L. 2002. Die Afrikaner en die naweë van die Anglo-Boereoorlog: Oorwonne of oorwinnaar. *Joernaal vir Eietydse Geskiedenis.* Vol. 27, No. 2.

Beak, G.B. 1906. *The Aftermath of War.* London: Edward Arnold.

Belfield, E. 1975. *The Boer War.* London: Leo Cooper.

Bellairs, L. 1972. *The Transvaal War 1880–1881.* Cape Town: Struik.

Bester, R.C. 2003. *Small Arms of the Anglo-Boer War 1899–1902.* Brandfort: Kraal Publishers.

Bester, R.C. 2016. The Small Arms of the Boer Republics: Their Acquisition, Use and Influence from 1880 to 1918. D. Phil thesis. University of the Free State, Bloemfontein.

Blake, A. 2012. *Boereverraaier – Teregstellings tydens die Anglo-Boereoorlog.* Cape Town: Tafelberg.

Blake, A. 2015. *Ontsnap – Boerekrygsgevangenes se strewe na vryheid.* Cape Town: Tafelberg.

Breytenbach, J.H. 1969. *Die geskiedenis van die Tweede Vryheidsoorlog – Vol. 1 en II.* Pretoria: Government Printer.

Breytenbach, J.H. and Ploeger, J. 1980. *Majuba gedenkboek.* Roodepoort: Cum Books.

Bridgeland, T. 1998. *Field Gun Jack versus the Boers – The Royal Navy in South Africa.* Barnsley: Leo Cooper.

Briggs, L. 1901. *The Staff Work of the Anglo-Boer War.* London: Grant Richards.

Carruthers, J., Cuthbertson, G., Gray, S., et al. (eds) *The Jameson Raid – A Centennial Retrospective.* Johannesburg: The Brenthurst Press.

Changuion, L. 2000. Die lewe in die Suid-Afrikaanse Boerekrygsgevangenekampe tydens die Anglo-Boereoorlog 1899–1902. Unpublished MA dissertation. University of Pretoria, Pretoria.

Changuion, L. 2001. *Silence of the Guns, The History of the Long Toms of the Anglo-Boer War.* Pretoria: Protea.

Changuion, L., Jacobs, F. and Alberts, P. 2003. *Suffering of War – A Photographic Portrayal of the Suffering in the Anglo-Boer War.* Brandfort: Kraal Publishers.

Changuion, L. and Steenkamp, B. 2000. *Omstrede land.* Paper presented at the War Museum, 2000.

Churchill, W.S. 1900. *London to Ladysmith via Pretoria.* London: Longmans Green.

Cloete, P.G. 2000. *The Anglo-Boer War, A Chronology.* Pretoria: J.P. van der Walt.

Collins, C. 1965. *Free Statia – Reminiscences of a Lifetime in the Orange Free State, vol. XII W.* Cape Town: Struik.

Comparato, F.E. 1965. *Age of Great Guns.* Harrisburg (PA): The Stackpole Company.

Constantine, R., Van Zyl, J. and Pretorius, T. 2014. *Gedenkuitgawe – Wedervaringe van vroue en kinders in konsentrasiekampe en te velde gedurende die Anglo-Boereoorlog 1899-1902.* Bloemfontein: Firefly Publications.

Creswicke, L. 1900. *South Africa and the Transvaal War.* Cape Town: D.E. M'Connell & Co.

Crisp, R. 1964. *The Outlanders – The Men who Made Johannesburg.* London: P. Davies.

Danzinger, C. 1978. *The Jameson Raid.* Cape Town: Macdonald South Africa.

D'Assonville, V.E. 2005. *Majuba.* Pretoria: Marnix.

Davenport, T.R.H. 1991. *South Africa – A Modern History.* London: Macmillan.

Davitt, M. 1902. *The Boer Fight for Freedom.* New York (NY): Funk & Wagnalls.

De Jesus, A. and Allen, J. 2014. *Re-envisioning the Anglo-Boer (South African) War.* Bloemfontein: Johannes Stegmann Art Gallery.

De Kock, W.J. 1976. *Suid-Afrikaanse biografiese woordeboek, deel I.* Cape Town: Tafelberg.

De Kock, W.J. and Kruger, D.W. 1972. *Suid-Afrikaanse biografiese woordeboek, deel II.* Cape Town: Tafelberg.

De Quesada, A.M. 2006. *Uniforms of the German Soldier (1870–WW1).* London: Greenhill Books.

De Villebois-Mareuil, G., Rossouw, J. and Botes, D.P.M. 2000. *Oorlogsdagboek van veggeneraal De Villebois-Mareuil.* Pretoria: Protea.

De Villiers, J.C. 2008. *Healers, Helpers and Hospitals – A History of Military Medicine in the Anglo-Boer War.* Pretoria: Protea.

De Villiers J.L. 1903. *Hoe ik ontsnapte: Verhaal van een merkwaardige ontsnapping van een Boer uit Engelsch-India.* Amsterdam: Hoveker en Wormser.

De Wet, C.R. 1985. *Three Years War.* Johannesburg: Scripta Africana.

De Wet, C.R. 1999. *Die Stryd tussen Boer en Brit.* Cape Town: Tafelberg.

Doyle, A.C. 1900. *The Great Boer War.* London: Smith, Elder & Co.

Du Toit, K. 2010. *Geskiedenis van die SA boerperd.* Pretoria: West Publishers.

Duxbury, G.R. 1981. *David & Goliath – The First War of Independence 1880–1881.* Pretoria: SA Museum of Military History.

Engelbrecht, C.L. 1987. *Geld in Suid-Afrika.* Cape Town: Tafelberg.

Ferreira, O.J.O. 2000. *Viva os Boers – Boeregeïnterneerdes in Portugal tydens die Anglo-Boereoorlog 1899–1902.* Pretoria: Protea.

Friend, D.G. 1993. Uniforms of the Staatsartillerie: Influences and Developments. *SA Military History Journal.* Vol. 9, No. 4.

Goosen, J.C. 1973. *Ons vloot – Die eerste vyftig jaar.* Cape Town: W.J. Flesch and partners.

Grundlingh, A.M. 1979. *Die hensoppers en joiners.* Pretoria and Cape Town: Haum Publishers.

Grundlingh, A. and Nasson, B. (eds). 2013. *Die oorlog kom huis toe.* Cape Town: Tafelberg.

Hall, D.D. 1971. Guns in South Africa 1899–1902, Part 1 to 5. *SA Military History Journal*. Vol. 2, No. 1–3.

Hall, D.D. 1999. *The Hall Handbook of the Anglo-Boer War*. Pietermaritzburg: University of KwaZulu-Natal Press.

Heunis, M.C. 2006. *Field Telegraphy in the Free State Artillery*. O.V.S.A.C. Study no.18, Oct.–Dec. 2006.

Heunis, M.C. 2008. *Boer War Commando Cuisine*. O.V.S.A.C. Study no.14, Jul.–Sep. 2008.

Heunis, M.C. and Wolfaardt, J. 2004. *"Mijn Pijp, Mijn Pijp" A Re-enactor's Guide to Boer War Smoking*. O.V.S.A.C. Study no.10, Oct.–Dec. 2004.

Hodgson, P. 1974. *Early War Photographs*. London: Osprey.

Hole, H.M. 1973. *The Jameson Raid*. Bulawayo: Books of Rhodesia.

In Memoriam N.Z.A.S.M., Dutch South African Railway Company. 1909. Amsterdam: De Bussy.

Judd, D. 1977. *The Boer War*. London: Hart-Davis, MacGibbon.

Kaighin, B. 1999. *A Diary of the Siege of Ladysmith*. Ladysmith: Brian Kaighin.

Karlsgodt, E.C. 2011. *Defending National Treasures: French Art and Heritage under Vichy*. Stanford (CA): Stanford University Press.

Kestell, J.D. 1920. *Christiaan De Wet – 'n Lewensbeskrywing*. Cape Town: De Nationale Pers.

Kotzé, D.J. 2010. *Dapper kinders van Suid-Afrika*. Pretoria: Protea.

Kruger, D.W. and Beyers, C.J. 1976. *Suid-Afrikaanse biografiese woordeboek, deel III*. Cape Town: Tafelberg.

Kruger, R. 1959. *Good-bye Dolly Gray*. London: Cassel.

Lastovica, E. and Lastovica, A. 1982. *Bottles and Bygones*. Cape Town: Don Nelson.

Lee, E. 1985. *To the Bitter End – A Photographic History of the Boer War 1899–1902*. London: Penguin.

Magnus, P. 1958. *Kitchener – Portrait of an Imperialist*. London: Butler & Tanner.

Manfred, N. 1941. *Paul Kruger – His Life and Times*. Durban: Knox.

Marais, P. 1993. *Penkoppe van die Tweede Vryheidsoorlog 1899–1902*. Pretoria: J.P. van der Walt & Son.

Marrion, R.J. 1989. Orange Free State Artillery. *Military Modelling*. June 1989.

Martin, D. 1988. *Duelling with Long Toms*. London: Impression Print.

McCarthy, Steve. 2013. Windows into History: 'Blended' photographs from the battlefields of KwaZulu-Natal. *Military History Journal*. Vol. 16, No. 1.

Meintjies, J. 1969. *Sword in the Sand*. Cape Town: Tafelberg.

Meintjies, J. 1970. *General Louis Botha – a Biography*. London: Cassell.

Meyers, E.M. 1986. Uniforms van die staatspresidentswag – herkoms en tradisie. *Militaria*. Vol. 16, No. 5.

Muller, C.E.J. 1969. *500 jaar Suid-Afrikaanse geskiedenis*. Cape Town and Pretoria: Academica.

Oosthuizen, S.P.R. 1975. Die beheer, behandeling en lewe van die krygsgevangenes gedurende die Anglo-Boereoorlog, 1899–1902. Unpublished D. Phil thesis. University of the Orange Free State, Bloemfontein.

Pakenham, T. 1979. *The Boer War*. London: Weidenfeldt and Nicolson.

Penning, L. 1902. *Verdedigers en verdrukkers der Afrikaansche vrijheid – karakterschetsen van mannen van beteekenis uit de Engelsch-Zuid-Afrikaanschen Oorlog 1899-1902*. 'S-Gravenhage: J.N. Verhoeve.

Ploeger, J. 1968. The Fortifications of Pretoria. *Military Historical and Archival Services Publication No. 1*. Pretoria: Government Printer.

Preller, G.S. 1925. *Historiese opstelle*. Pretoria: Van Schaik.

Preller, G.S. 1937. *Daglemier in Suid-Afrika*. Pretoria: Wallachs.

Pretorius, F. 1985. *1899–1902 Die Anglo-Boereoorlog*. Cape Town: Don Nelson.

Pretorius, F. 2001. *Scorched Earth*. Cape Town: Human & Rousseau.

Pretorius, F. (ed.). 2012. *Geskiedenis van Suid-Afrika – Van voortye tot vandag*. Cape Town: Tafelberg.

Pretorius, J.L. 1910. Ons Suidafrikaanse Militaire Tradisie. *Die Brandwag*. 28 June.

Raal, S. 1938. *Met die Boere in die veld*. Cape Town: Nasionale Pers.

Raath, A.W.G. 2002. *Die Boervrou, 1899-1902 Deel 2: Kampsmarte*. Bloemfontein: Volkskomitee vir die Herdenking van die Tweede Vryheidsoorlog.

Raath, A.W.G. 2007. *De la Rey – 'n Stryd vir vryheid en reg*. Brandfort: Kraal Publishers.

Ralph, J. 1900. *Towards Pretoria*. New York (NY): Frederick A. Stokes.

Reichmann, C. 1987. *Boer War Operations in South Africa, 1899–1901*. Melville: Scripta Africana.

Rothmann, F.L. 1947. *Oorlogsdagboek van 'n Transvaalse burger te velde*. Cape Town: Nasionale Boekhandel.

Schnurr, T. 1999. Imperial German Pickelhaube Evolution 1842–1915 in *Kaiser Bunker*. See http://www.kaisersbunker.com/pe/, accessed on 16 March 2017.

Schoeman, K. 2010. *Bloemfontein – Die ontstaan van 'n stad, 1846–1946*. Cape Town: Human & Rousseau.

Sellers, W.E.S. 1900. *From Aldershot to Pretoria*. London: The Religious Tract Society.

Sharp, G. 1976. *The Siege of Ladysmith*. Cape Town: Purnell & Sons.

Skennerton, I.D. 1987. *The British Service Lee: Lee-Metford and Lee-Enfield Rifles & Carbines*. Margate: Skennerton.

Smurthwaite, D. 1999. *Hamlyn History – The Boer War 1899–1902*. London: Octopus Publishing Group.

Solka, M. 2004. *German Armies 1870–1871 (1): Prussia (Men-at-arms)*. Oxford: Osprey.

St Leger, S.E. 1903. *War Sketches in Colour*. London: Adam & Charles Black.

Steenkamp, J.A. 1980. Die Vrystaatse vrywillige militêre eenhede 1854–1899. *Militaria*. Vol. 10, No. 1.

Swart, C.R. 1961. *Kinders van Suid-Afrika*. Bloemfontein: Nasionale Pers.

Swemmer, T.P.E. 1953. *Die geskiedenis van die Vrystaatse Artillerie*. MA dissertation. University of the Orange Free State, Bloemfontein.

Symons, J. 1974. *Bullers Campaign*. London: White Lion.

The Centre for Photographic Conservation. 1992. *The Imperfect Image; Photographs – Their Past, Present and Future*. London: The Centre for Photographic Conservation.

Time-Life Books. 1970. *The Camera: Life Library of Photography*. New York (NY): Time-Life Books.

Todd, P. and Fordham, D. 1980. *Private Tucker's Boer War Diary*. London: Elm Tree Books.

Van Bart, M. and Scholtz, L. 2003. *Vir vryheid en reg*. Cape Town: Tafelberg.

Van der Bank, D.A. 1993. Die stryd om die behoud van die identiteit van die Afrikaner in die Oranjerivier-kolonie, 1902–1910. D. Phil thesis. University of the Orange Free State, Bloemfontein.

Van der Merwe, F. 2000. *Perde van die Anglo-Boereoorlog*. Kleinmond: Kleinmond.

Van der Merwe, F. 2013. *Sport in die Boerekrygsgevangekampe tydens die Anglo-Boereoorlog 1899–1902*. Stellenbosch: F.J.G. Publications.

Van der Merwe, N.J. 1921. *Marthinus Theunis Steyn, 'n Lewensbeskrywing, Deel 1 en 2*. Cape Town: De Nasionale Pers.

Van der Merwe, N.J. 1926. *Die Nasionale Vrouemonument*. Bloemfontein: Die Sentrale Pers.

Van Schoor, M.C.E. 1973. *De Wet en sy verkenners*. Elsiesrivier: Suid-Afrikaanse Uitsaaikorporasie.

Van Schoor, M.C.E. 2005. *Die Bittereinder vrede*. Brandfort: Kraal Publishers.

Van Schoor, M.C.E., Coetzee, C.G. and Rapportryerskorps Pretoria-Tuine. 1982. *Kampkinders 1900–1902*. Bloemfontein: War Museum of the Boer Republics.

Van Zyl, P.H.S. 1944. *Die Helde-album van ons vryheidstryd*. Johannesburg: Die Afrikaanse Pers-boekhandel.

Venter, E.A. 1982. *Ons geskiedenisalbum*. Potchefstroom: Klerksdorp Record.

Viljoen, B.J. 1902. *My Reminiscences of the Anglo-Boer War*. London: Hood, Douglas, & Howard.

Von Heister, C. 1901. The Orange Free State Artillery. *Journal of the United Service Institute*. Vol. xlv, July to December 1901, No. 276. London: S.W. Whitehall, JJ Keller & Co.

Walmsley, A.B. 1964. Staats Artillerie van de O.V.S. Uniform and Organization. *Africana Notes and News*. Vol.16, No.4.

Wessels, E. 2002. *Veldslae: Anglo-Boereoorlog 1899–1902*. Pretoria: Lapa Publishers.

Wessels, E. 2010. *Banneling in die vreemde*. Centurion: Kraal Publishers.

Wessels, E. and Heunis, V. 2010. Die Kantskool by Koppies. *Knapsak*. Vol. 22, No. 1.

Wessels, E. and Raath, A.W.G. 2012. *Onthou – Kronieke van vroue- en kinderlyding, 1899–1902*. Centurion: Kraal Publishers.

Williams, J.R. 1982. Artillery Corps of the Orange Free State. *The Military Historical Society*. Vol. 33, No. 129.

Wilson, H.W. 1900–1902. *With the Flag to Pretoria, vol. 1 and 2*. London: Harmsworth Brothers.

Wilson, S. 1909. *South African Memories*. London: Edward Arnold.

Women's Memorial Centenary Collection. 2013. *Universal Suffering during the South African War 1899–1902*. Bloemfontein: War Museum of the Boer Republics.

Worsfold, W.B. 1906. *Lord Alfred Milner's Work in SA*. London: John Murray.

DOCUMENTS

Commandant-general and Secretary of State: Incoming letters, accession number unknown, Pretoria National Archive, 1882–1899.

Diary of an unknown citizen about the Siege of Mafeking, document collection: accession number 6340/3, War Museum of the Boer Republics.

Diary of SJ Roos kept during her stay in the Bethulie concentration camp (April 1901–November 1902), document collection: accession number 06455/00001, War Museum of the Boer Republics.

Fact sheet about Jurgens Albertus Nieman's death and the clothes he had on, document collection: accession number 06680/00004, War Museum of the Boer Republics.

Notulen, verrichtingen van de Conferentie 31 Mei 1899 en volgende dagen te Bloemfontein: accession number 04956/00010, Staatsdrukkerrij van de ZAR.

Payrolls of the OVSAC (1890–1898), accession number unknown, Free State Archive.

Projects of the War Museum 2011: accession number 7433/9, War Museum of the Boer Republics.

Staatskoerant no. 2307 of 21 December 1920, Union of South Africa government gazette, 24 December 1920.

War Office-documentation, Public Records Office – Kew London and Pretoria National Archive.

NEWSPAPERS

Cape Argus, 18 October 1899.

Los Angeles Herald, no. 37, 7 November 1900.

Midland News and Karoo Farmer, 15 November 1899.

WEBSITES

http://angloboerwarmuseum.com/Boer04_mysteries.html

http://www.bwm.org.au/site/Horses.asp

http://www.kaisersbunker.com/pe/

http://www.saboerperd.com/

http://www.theinfolist.com/php/SummaryGet.php?FindGo=Transvaalse Staatsartillerie

Electronic prisoners of war data lists, War Museum of the Boer Republics, http://www.wmbr.org.za/view.asp?pg=research&pgsub=databases&head1=Search

Index